RUNES FOR BEGINNERS

A Guide to Reading Runes in Divination, Rune Magic, and the Meaning of the Elder Futhark Runes

LISA CHAMBERLAIN

Runes for Beginners

Published by **Chamberlain Publications**

ISBN-13: 978-1-912715-01-5

Disclaimer

No part of this publication may be reproduced or transmitted in any form or by any means, mechanical or electronic, including photocopying or recording, or by any information storage and retrieval system, or transmitted by email without permission in writing from the publisher.

While all attempts have been made to verify the information provided in this publication, neither the author nor the publisher assumes any responsibility for errors, omissions, or contrary interpretations of the subject matter herein.

This book is for entertainment purposes only. The views expressed are those of the author alone, and should not be taken as expert instruction or commands. The reader is responsible for his or her own actions.

Adherence to all applicable laws and regulations, including international, federal, state, and local governing professional licensing, business practices, advertising, and all other aspects of doing business in the US, Canada, or any other jurisdiction is the sole responsibility of the purchaser or reader.

Neither the author nor the publisher assumes any responsibility or liability whatsoever on the behalf of the purchaser or reader of these materials.

Any perceived slight of any individual or organization is purely unintentional.

YOUR FREE GIFT

Thank you for adding this book to your Wiccan library! To learn more, why not join Lisa's Wiccan community and get an exclusive, free spell book?

The book is a great starting point for anyone looking to try their hand at practicing magic. The ten beginner-friendly spells can help you to create a positive atmosphere within your home, protect yourself from negativity, and attract love, health, and prosperity.

Little Book of Spells is now available to read on your laptop, phone, tablet, Kindle or Nook device!

To download, simply visit the following link:

www.wiccaliving.com/bonus

GET A FREE AUDIOBOOK
FROM LISA CHAMBERLAIN

Did you know that all of Lisa's books are available in audiobook format? Best of all, you can get **an audiobook of your choice completely free** as part of a 30-day trial with Audible.

If you'd like to learn divination, check out Lisa's *Runes for Beginners*, which covers the origins and meanings of these ancient mystical symbols, including their divinatory interpretations and their uses in magic. Download for free here:

www.wiccaliving.com/free-runes-audiobook

Or, if you'd like to learn another form of divination, try Lisa's best-selling *Tarot for Beginners*. The updated 2nd edition of this best-selling book covers the origins of Tarot, a comprehensive overview of the 78 cards and their meanings, and tips for beginning readers. Simply visit:

www.wiccaliving.com/free-tarot-audiobook

Audible members receive free audiobooks every month, as well as exclusive discounts. It's a great way to experiment and see if audiobook learning works for you.

If you're not satisfied, you can cancel anytime within the trial period. You won't be charged, and you can still keep your books!

CONTENTS

8

INTRODUCTION

To the average person, the various symbols that make up what we call "the runes" may be seen simply as archaic remnants of a primitive and long-abandoned alphabet. However, those who work with these mystical symbols in divination and other forms of magic know that they are far more.

Although the runes have not been in widespread use for several centuries, the past few decades have seen quite a revival of interest in runic magic and divination. You may have seen a set of runes in "New Age" or other magical shops, likely nestled next to various Tarot decks and other divination supplies. Or perhaps you've come across spells in Wiccan books that call for carving specific runes into a candle. If you're a fan of J.R.R. Tolkien, you're bound to be familiar with some of these symbols, which appeared in his novel *The Hobbit* and inspired the invented "runic" alphabet in *The Lord of the Rings*. But what are runes, exactly?

In the academic sense, the runes are known as the characters in a group of alphabets used to write in various languages spoken by the Germanic peoples of Europe, during a period starting roughly in the first century B.C.E. and ending several hundred years later. As Christianity spread throughout the regions occupied by the Germanic peoples, the runes were gradually replaced by the letters we know today as the Latin alphabet.

However, unlike our modern letters, the runic symbols had been in use for magical purposes long before they were fashioned into a writing system. The runes carried deep meanings for the people who used them, and for this reason they never disappeared completely, even once they were outlawed by the Christian Church. After spending a few centuries in relative obscurity, the runes were eventually revived by various scholars and mystics, and ultimately transcended their Germanic origins to become part of various spiritual systems in the 20th century.

Today, many who work with runes practice reconstructionist versions of ancient Germanic religion, such as Asatru and Heathenry, or more eclectic forms of what is often called Northern Tradition Paganism. These practices focus on the deities, beliefs, and customs of the ancient Germanic peoples, with varying degrees of adherence to what is actually known about these cultures in pre-Christian times.

However, it is not necessary to be oriented to Germanic practices in order to forge a working relationship with runic symbols, as their magical energies and communicative abilities are universal. Many people who work with runes have very little, if any, connection to the Northern European ancestors who handed them down to us. Nonetheless, it is important to have a basic appreciation and respect for the origins of these magical symbols if you want to use them well.

So who were the "Germanic peoples"? "Germanic" is a very broad term that refers to many different ancient tribes, with a wide range of cultural identities and geographical locations (including, but not limited to, what we know today as Germany). The link between these various groups is in the languages they spoke, rather than any single ethnic makeup or central belief system.

Like the ancient Celts, the Germanic tribes migrated thousands of years ago from one area of Europe, expanding from the north into the western and central parts of the continent. By the first century B.C.E., they had reached the borders of the Roman Empire, where their customs were described in writing, for the first time, by Roman scribes.

Other knowledge of the various pre-Christianized Germanic tribes comes from archeological evidence, mythology, and other literature from Scandinavia and Britain, two other main regions occupied by these groups. It is from these sources that we can discover the magical uses for the runes among the Germanic peoples. However, no complete picture of these practices exists, and we are left to our own magical intuition to fill in the details as needed.

In this guide, you will be introduced to the history of the runes and their significance within the framework of the Germanic magical worldview. However, the practices described within are not meant to be representative of contemporary Germanic Neopagan spiritual systems such as Asatru, Heathenry, or Northern Traditional Paganism. Instead, this introductory guide approaches the runes from the perspective of a more general, eclectic Craft practice.

A minimal degree of magical experience on the part of the reader is assumed, but is not required in order to benefit from the information within. You'll learn basic techniques of rune magic and divination, as well as the divinatory meanings and magical uses of the runes. (This guide uses the Elder Futhark runes—the oldest known runic alphabet—but the knowledge you gain from these pages can be applied to any set of runes.)

As you read and experiment with the information within, be sure stay in touch with your intuition, as this is the only way to truly develop your skills in any form of magic. Enjoy your journey into the world of the runes!

PART ONE

WHAT ARE RUNES?

WHISPERS, SECRETS, AND MYSTERIES

The enigmatic nature of the runes is undeniable. As symbols, they mean little (if anything) to the untrained eye, yet they still seem to suggest some kind of ancient mystic significance. And while we may unlock their mysteries to some degree through learning about and working with runes, even the most adept students of their magical properties and divinatory meanings will find there is always more to discover.

There is just something inherently esoteric about these ancient written characters. This is even evident in the meanings you'll find for the word "rune" in today's dictionaries—while they are primarily identified as both letters and divination symbols, runes are also defined as "mystery," "magic," and even "spells or incantations."

The English word "rune" comes to us from the Norse word *runa*, which means "a secret," or "to whisper." However, we also find words related to "rune" in several old Northern European languages in both Germanic and Celtic cultures, all of which have similar interpretations: the Old Norse word *rún*, meaning "a secret" or "mystery"; the Old Irish *rún* and Middle Welsh *rhin*, also translated variously as "mystery," "secret" or "whisper"; and the Scots word *roun*, meaning "to whisper" or "to speak much and often about one thing."

The Norse *runa* is also the root for the English word we use to identify a very magical tree: the rowan. Found throughout Northern Europe, the rowan tree has long been sacred to various magical traditions and is used widely for protection. It is known by many folk names, including "rune tree" and "whisper tree."

Some scholars trace the word "rune" back even further to the prehistoric Proto-Indo-European language, which is believed to be the ancestor of many later ancient languages. These linguistic roots pre-date the use of runic characters for writing, which tells us that runes belonged to the world of mystery and magic well before they became a system of writing. Indeed, as we will see throughout this guide, their role as a means of ordinary communication barely scratches the surface of what these ancient symbols were—and still are—capable of.

In the discussions below, we'll take a brief look at the known history of the runes, including their origins and evolutions as a writing system, their mundane and magical uses in ancient Germanic culture, and their fate during the Christianization of Northern Europe. Then we'll explore the deeper, esoteric realms of the runes through their appearances in ancient Norse literature. Finally, we'll meet the runes of the Elder Futhark, the oldest known runic script and the one most often used by rune workers and other magicians today.

ANCIENT INNOVATIONS: HOW THE RUNES CAME INTO BEING

Modern writing systems, or "alphabets," as we know them, are a relatively recent invention in the history of human beings, having only emerged around 1700 B.C.E.. Before that, written communication took place in the form of symbols such as pictographs and ideographs, which stood for objects and abstract concepts rather than the sounds used to pronounce words aloud.

Many of these symbols have been found in European caves and on rock carvings, with some dating as far back as 12,000 to 17,000 years ago. In Sweden and other parts of Scandinavia, many of the signs on these rock carvings have been recognized as "prerunic" symbols which were later integrated into the runic writing system. (Other signs from this period, such as the sunwheel and the cross, were not adapted as runic letters but are thought to have had magical significance.)

As ancient societies evolved, trade expanded well beyond the borders of local communities and economies became more complex. Different cultures interacting with each other through trade and migration brought new words into their languages, which there were no corresponding symbols for. For these and other reasons, written script began to replace ideographs.

The process began in ancient Egypt, where a system of letters—characters which stand for a sound rather than an object or idea—was created as a more efficient means of writing than the hieroglyphic system. Out of this new letter-based system eventually came the Phoenician alphabet, which was standardized and spread to other areas of North Africa and across the Mediterranean to southern Europe.

The Phoenician alphabet in turn gave rise to the ancient Greek alphabet (which is actually where we get the word "alphabet," by combining the first two letters of the Greek writing system—alpha and beta). The Greek alphabet was then adapted by the Etruscan civilization on the Italian peninsula. Several other Greek-derived script-based systems also arose in this region of Europe, grouped together under the name "Old Italic." It is believed that one of these alphabets, often referred to as "North Italic," was used to create the runic script of the Germanic tribes.

This North Italic origin has not yet been firmly agreed upon by all scholars, but it is the most plausible of the existing theories at this point. Although Italy is nowhere near Scandinavia, where much of the surviving evidence of rune use is found, there were Germanic tribes living in the Alps of central Europe, where Etruscan merchants had established trading routes. Evidence that these two cultures intermingled is found on helmets from this region dating back to around 300 B.C.E., with inscriptions in North Italic script that honor Germanic gods.

At some point between then and the first century C.E., some form of Old Italic was synthesized with several pre-runic symbols to create the first runic "alphabet," for the purpose of representing the sounds of the Germanic language. This new system was then passed along from tribe to tribe throughout the Germanic regions, including all the way up to the coast of the North Sea and the farther reaches of Scandinavia.

MESSAGES AND MAGIC

As the runic system was integrated into Germanic culture, people began using these symbols for various types of inscriptions, as early as the first century C.E.. From artifacts such as spears, shields, rock carvings and giant stones, we know that the runes were used for many purposes, including magic.

Runic inscriptions on weaponry and jewelry turned these objects into talismans. Memorial stones were inscribed to commemorate the deceased—much like modern grave stones, but for the direct purpose of ensuring the deceased's safe passage to the afterlife. Some carvings consisted of what we might recognize as spellwork today, such as magical formulas, prayers, invocations, and symbol magic.

As for divination—one of the main uses of the runes today—there is evidence suggesting that at least some ancient Germanic people also used runes for this purpose. The most frequently cited source is the Roman author Tacitus, who described a divination process in his book *Germania* in the first century C.E..

People seeking answers from the invisible realms would carve symbols into strips of wood cut from the branch of a fruit-bearing tree. The carved strips were then scattered onto a white cloth. The reader of the signs would pick up three of the strips while looking upward "toward heaven," so as to be sure to choose at random, with the gods' guidance. If the divination was publicly held, the reader was the community priest. In private readings, the male head of the family would choose and interpret the symbols.

Some scholars are skeptical as to whether this was actually runic divination, since Tacitus does not call the symbols "runes," and since the runic system may not have been quite developed yet by the time of his writing. Another source—the 9th-century C.E. *Vita Ansgari* by the Christian writer Rimbert—contains accounts of divination in Scandinavia that likely involved runes, but Rimbert uses the term "drawing lots."

However, "drawing lots" was actually a different kind of divination, used to distribute land among community members in parts of Northern Europe, rather than to discover hidden knowledge. So it's possible that Rimbert—and Tacitus before him—simply didn't use the terminology that the Germanic people themselves would have used. In any case, once the runic script came into use throughout Germanic lands, it is believed that runes were adopted into divination customs that had already been in place.

In later centuries, runes were also used for mundane writing purposes, such as documents related to business and law, and personal messages, including love letters! Many of these messages were carved into sticks and carried from person to person until they reached their destination. Runes didn't appear in written form on actual parchment until around the 14th century C.E..

By this time, however, the Latin alphabet had essentially taken over, and little evidence of runes written with ink and quill remains. Nonetheless, people still used runes for writing, and in remote areas of Scandinavia this practice lasted even into the 20th century. Other non-magical uses continued as well, such as in runic calendars—perpetual calendars often carved in wood or bone—which were household items in Scandinavia until well into the 18th century.

Although Christianity had come to Northern Europe by the 11th century, native Germanic magical practices hung on, and lasted in some places for several hundred more years. In Iceland, a magical grimoire known as the *Galdrabók,* compiled during the 16th and 17th centuries, included rune work. In the Black Forest region of what is now Germany, runic symbols continued to be incorporated into magical designs on farm buildings—a practice that traveled to the United States with Germanic immigrants in the 1800s.

But by and large, Christianization had driven native religious traditions throughout Europe underground, if not stomping them out completely, by the 15th century. As for the runes, their magical significance was clearly obvious to the Church, as their use was banned repeatedly during the Middle Ages. Nonetheless, runes remained part of the fabric of the collective Germanic psyche, refusing to disappear altogether.

RUNIC REVIVALS

Thankfully, it wasn't too long before the mysterious rock carvings and other remnants of the age of runes caught the attention of scholars in Scandinavian lands. During the 1600s, Johannes Bureus traveled throughout Sweden to collect and record runic inscriptions and wrote three books on the runes. Though he was an academic who considered himself a Christian, Bureus was also interested in learning the magical significance of these symbols, and ultimately created a magical system that was something of a blend between authentic native Germanic rune lore and the Christian version of the Kabbalah. A few other scholars also explored the runes around this time, but it wasn't until the European Romantic period of the late 18th and early 19th centuries that a true runic "revival" became possible.

During this time, interest in native Germanic folklore and culture was being revitalized, as evidenced by the Gothic League in Sweden, which sought to reconnect with the pre-Christian worldview by working with ancient Scandinavian literature, where the runes frequently appear. Further south, the brothers Jacob and Wilhelm Grimm (of fairy tale fame) began collecting ancient Germanic folk tales, and Wilhelm took a particular interest in uncovering the history of rune use in this region.

Through these and other efforts, the pagan tradition of the Germanic peoples was elevated to a level of academic inquiry, and was no longer seen as an existential threat to Christianity. This shift paved the way for a later Germanic "Renaissance" (also known as "Pan-Germanism") in the late 19th and early 20th centuries, during which some modern mystics and occultists truly worked to revive the runes according to their original magical purposes.

The most widely credited figure in this runic revival was Guido von List, a prolific Austrian writer and mystic whose studies led him to create a new runic script called the Armanen runes. List believed these runes to be the most ancient Germanic script, and that they had been revealed to him intuitively while he was recovering from a cataract surgery that left him temporarily blind.

It later became clear that the Armanen runes were definitely a modern adaptation, but that didn't diminish List's influence on the study of runes in Germany and Austria, and his Armanen runes are still used by many Neopagans today. The esoteric groups associated with List remained active after his death in 1919, as interest in Germanic history and religion continued within the region.

Unfortunately, the larger Pan-Germanic movement fed into the development of German nationalism and the rise of the Nazi party, which essentially coopted the runes in their symbolism. Those rune workers and mystics who did not fall in line with Nazi ideology were outlawed and often executed, while the Nazis, through their horrific actions, went on to destroy the positive reputation that the runes and Germanic paganism in general had gained by that time. Fortunately, the Germanic deities, magical lore, and the runes themselves were later adopted into other esoteric movements in Europe that were fairly universal in scope, incorporating occult elements from throughout the ancient world.

Finally, in the late 20th century, as Neopaganism in many forms (including Wicca) began to spread rapidly through Europe and North America, the runes came to the attention of English-speaking occultists. The first person to publish an introduction to the runes in English was Ralph Blum in 1983, followed very closely by Edred Thorsson in 1984.

These two writers differ drastically in terms of esoteric philosophy and attention to historical accuracy, with Thorsson anchoring his work within the cultural framework of pagan Scandinavia, and Blum essentially intuiting the meanings of the runes entirely, through a lens of both Christian and East Asian influences. Of course, in our modern era, the runes (along with Germanic paganism in general) have been a topic of interest and sometimes fierce debate among many writers, scholars, Neopagans, and other occultists, just as they have been for centuries.

This brief overview summarizes what we know about the origin and development of the runes from available historical sources. However, we also know that the esoteric significance, meanings, and magical uses of these symbols have a history far older than the development of the runic writing system. After all, as we have seen above, the etymology of the word "rune" is actually older than the languages used by the ancient Germanic peoples.

Indeed, according to Norse mythology, the runes have existed since the beginning of time—even before the birth of the gods. Let's take a look now at some of the tales that remain from those ancient days, and what they have to tell us about the mystery and magic of the runes.

TIMELESS SYMBOLS: RUNES IN NORSE MYTHOLOGY

Although the runes were in use throughout the areas of Europe occupied by Germanic tribes, the only written accounts we have today of their mythical origins come from the Nordic region. Because Christianization and the eradication of native religions occurred a few centuries later in the northern-most parts of the continent than in the rest of Europe, the Scandinavians had more time to preserve their history and beliefs in writing than their southern counterparts did.

Much of the source material regarding Norse mythology and religion comes from Iceland, in the form of collections of stories and poems that were handed down over the centuries and finally recorded sometime between the ninth and fourteenth centuries C.E.. The two most significant sources are the Prose Edda and the Poetic Edda— stories and poems that tell of the gods and goddesses of the Germanic pantheon. Other sources, such as historical works and sagas, also shed light on the worldview of the ancient Norse.

Unlike the Norse deities, and even the world itself, the runes have no origin story in the recorded myths. That is, there is no tale in which a specific being or force creates the runes. Instead, the runes are eternal—they have always existed, just like the two primordial worlds of fire (Muspelheim) and ice (Niflheim) that existed before the creation of the rest of the Universe.

The runes contain the secrets of the Universe, which can be glimpsed and even utilized by those who understand their meanings. In this way, they are somewhat akin to later magical and divination systems such as the Kabalah, the Hermetic Principles, and the Tarot: we can learn and manifest much from understanding them, but they still remain mysterious. They will never reveal *everything* there is to know, no matter how long or how diligently we study them.

FATE AND THE NORNS

Perhaps the best place to start a mythological exploration of the runes is with the giant tree known as Yggdrasill. This tree, usually said to be an ash tree but believed by some scholars to be a yew, is at the center of the Universe and holds the nine worlds of the Norse cosmology together in its roots and branches. Through Yggdrasill, all things are connected, and it is often referred to as "the World Tree."

At the bottom of Yggdrasill is the Well of Urd—also known as the Well of Fate—a bottomless pool where the gods are said to meet to hold their daily meetings. Also present at this well are the Norns— female beings from the realm of the giants (called *jötnar*). The Norns tend to Yggdrasill by protecting its roots and watering it with the sacred water from the Well of Urd.

The Norns are said to weave the tapestry of fate that all human beings—and gods—are intertwined within. More than any other beings in Norse mythology, the Norns influence the course of events large and small, as they spin, weave, and sever the threads of fate. In addition to their weaving, they also carve runes into the trunk of Yggsrasill. The meanings, or intentions, of the runes are carried up through the trunk and into the branches, and affect everything within the nine worlds that reside there, including Midgard, the world of human beings.

This role in shaping the destiny of the Universe belongs to the three named Norns—Urd, Verdandi, and Skuld—who are said to be sisters. (There are other norns, without the capital "N," who are said to arrive at the birth of each human being to influence (or "weave") their fate.) The names of the Norns, from Old Norse, translate roughly to concepts of past, present and future. Urd (the eldest sister) represents "What Once Was," Verdandi (the middle sister) represents "What Is

Coming into Being," and Skuld (the youngest) represents "What Shall Be."

It seems likely that the use of runes for divination is at least partly due to their connection with the Norns, the weavers of fate and the mythical embodiments of time. However, the concepts of "fate" and "time" in the Norse cosmology are not quite the same as the way we typically define them in modern culture, and this is important to understand when working divination with the runes.

When it comes to time, the Norse conception is cyclical. It is always in a process of renewal, rather than being strictly linear. As the present fades into the past, it becomes the "new" past, which means that the past never stays the same. Similarly, what happens in the present affects the future—the future does not exist independently of either past or present. A slightly different set of translations for the names of the Norns illustrates this idea: "That Which Is" (Urd), "That Which Is Becoming" (Verdandi) and "That Which Should Be" (Skuld). "Should be" is not the same thing as "will be," for the future is never concrete until it's actually the present.

In a similar sense, what we would call "fate" is not entirely set in stone, no matter what the Norns (or norns) have woven into a person's destiny at their birth. Although the Norns are credited in ancient Norse tales with causing both fortunate and tragic circumstances, a person (or a god) could learn to navigate unfolding events and adapt to changing circumstances in order to minimize risk or maximize good fortune.

Unlike the ancient Greek concept of fate, where no matter how much gods (and mortals) tried to avoid it, they always ultimately met their pre-determined destiny, the Norse concept allows for the present to affect the future. So while we do not have complete control over everything that happens in our lives, we are not completely helpless to change aspects of our fate, either.

This makes perfect sense when it comes to reading the runes—if there were no way to have any affect on future outcomes, then why bother with divination, or any other form of magic, in the first place?

ODIN'S DISCOVERY

Though the Norns have always had the use of the runes, these magical symbols were not available to the gods—and therefore not to humans either—until Odin discovered them through a great ordeal of self-sacrifice.

Odin is the central figure in Norse mythology, and is also referred to as "Allfather," as he is the father of the gods as well as the people. Unlike some other deities in these myths, Odin does not belong strictly to the Norse. To other Germanic tribes, he was known as Wodan (or Wotan). To the Anglo-Saxons, he was Woden, and seems to have been primarily a warrior god with a rather savage character. However, Woden is mentioned in the 10th-century Old English "Nine Herbs Charm," where he uses magical herbs to destroy a serpent, so it seems he had at least one other role in addition to leading the charge in battle.

The Norse Odin is similarly multi-skilled, and probably far more so, though without more written records from the Anglo-Saxons and other Germanic tribes, it's impossible to know for sure. Nevertheless, Odin is not only a warrior god and the father of gods and humans, but he is also associated with death and the afterlife, divination, inspiration, wisdom, healing, poetry, philosophy, and of course, magic.

Odin has many animal familiars, two of which are ravens named Huginn ("thought") and Muninn ("memory"). The ravens fly all over the world and bring back information to Odin, allowing him knowledge he could not gain otherwise. Huginn and Muninn form just one example of Odin's desire for knowledge, especially of the esoteric kind. Two stories in particular illustrate the lengths he was willing to go to in order to earn his reputation as a very wise and knowing god.

In the first story, Odin wishes to drink from Mimir's Well, also known as the "well of wisdom" or "fountain of wisdom." Mimir was a being who knew more about the universe than just about anyone, due to drinking from the well every day. Mimir tells Odin he may drink from the well, but only if he gives up one of his eyes. Odin does so, becoming the "one-eyed god," and gaining much wisdom from the sacrifice.

In the second story, Odin hears talk of the runes and wishes to discover and understand their mystical secrets, so he journeys to the Well of Urd where the runes reside. However, the runes are immensely powerful sources of magic and knowledge, and do not reveal themselves to just anybody—even a god. Odin knows that to gain the respect of the runes, he will again have to make a sacrifice. This time, he pierces himself with his sword and hangs himself upside down from a branch of the great tree Yggdrasill, overlooking the Well of Urd. He stays there, injured and upside down, for nine days and nights, not allowing any other gods to provide him with water, food, or any other kind of assistance. Finally, the runes—their shapes and their secrets—are revealed to him in the water below.

This story is often cited as an example of a shamanic initiation, in which a person (or, in this case, a god) undergoes a severe physical and/or psychological trial in order to gain knowledge of esoteric mysteries. Found in pagan cultures around the world, shamans were wisdom-keepers and healers who could travel to the invisible planes of existence to find solutions to the problems encountered by their communities. This ability was only gained through a transformative experience of self-sacrifice, often involving a metaphorical "dismemberment" of the body, such as we see in the story of Odin's eye at Mimir's well.

In the case of the runes, Odin puts himself through physical pain, deprivation, and psychological loneliness (hanging from the tree for nine days and nights) and is transformed by the knowledge of the runes. In the poem *Hávamál*, where this story is recorded, Odin tells us that after he lifted the runes from the Well of Urd, he "grew and waxed in wisdom," finding that he could now work great feats of magic. He can use his new magical knowledge to help himself and others escape danger, defeat enemies, heal from injuries and illness, and even find love.

RUNIC MASTERY

Throughout Norse literature, the runes are portrayed as powerful and even potentially dangerous magical tools. Access to their secrets is not granted easily—as we have seen from Odin's ordeal at the Well of Urd—nor are the runes simple to understand.

Odin may have been able to receive the knowledge of the runes somewhat instantly (that is, after his nine days and nights of self-sacrifice), but he was a god, and a god of wisdom, at that. When it comes to "mere mortals," it seems that at least some amount of study and discipline was required, along with a special aptitude for magical work. Those who pursued and successfully applied this knowledge were called "runemasters" and were greatly respected in Norse culture—particularly during the Viking era.

We see this in the Eddic poem known as *Rigsmál*, which tells how the "three classes" of human society (serfs, free peasants, and nobles) came to be. Here there is a strong association between nobility and mastery of the runes. The god Rig, who is more commonly known as Heimdall, fathers the first child of each of the classes—Thrall, the first serf (or slave); Churl, the first free peasant; and Jarl (or "Earl"), the first nobleman.

It is Jarl to whom Rig teaches the runes, once he is of an age to learn them. Jarl goes on to have several sons of his own, but the poem tells us that only the youngest of them—called "Kon" or "King"—knows the runes. This knowledge, and the ability to put it into practice through magical acts, gives this son special status within his family of nobles.

In the epic *Saga of the Volsungs*, runes are mentioned often and they play significant roles in some of the plots. In one chapter, we get a closer look at what "learning the runes" actually entailed as Brunhilde, a Valkyrie warrior maiden, teaches the runes to Sigurd, a mortal hero.

Sigurd has already learned at least something of the runes from his foster father, but Brunhilde holds even more knowledge, and goes into detail about different kinds of runes, their magical purposes, and how they should be carved, depending on the situation. For example, to ensure safe passage at sea, she instructs Sigurd to make "wave runes" and burn them onto the oar. There are several different kinds of runes grouped according to purpose, such as "victory runes," "speech runes," and "cure runes." These magical classifications are still observed by modern runemasters.

The Norse tales also warn that the power of the runes can cause unintended harm if used incorrectly, whether for written communication or for magic. Another story from the *Saga of the Volsungs* tells of a message sent from Gudrun, a member of the royal family, to her brothers, warning them of possible treachery. The message is intercepted and the runes altered, to make it appear as though Gudrun is inviting her brothers for a visit. The wife of one of the brothers inspects the message and is able to see the original message underneath the alteration. She warns her husband not to leave home, and says, "You cannot be very skilled at reading runes if you think your sister has asked you to come."

In a widely-cited story from *Egill's Saga*, the hero, Egill, visits a woman who has been seriously ill, and near her bed discovers a whale bone with runes carved into it as an attempt to cure her. But whoever carved them was not skilled in rune magic, and had actually made her worse. Egill, a Viking poet who is presumably much more talented with runes, carves the appropriate symbols into a piece of antler and leaves it under the woman's bed. She is cured almost instantly.

Indeed, the ability to simply know the runes and carve them legibly seems to have been held in high regard, as though the mere act of bringing the symbols into 3-dimensional manifestation was a powerful thing to do. We can see this from many Old Norse runic inscriptions which identify the person carving the runes, even when the message itself has little to do with the runemaster. This was common on the bauta stones that served as memorials to the deceased, which typically read something like "Olsen carved these runes in memory of _____."

The messages on such stones might or might not provide the name and/or biographical information about the deceased, but the carver of the runes was almost always named. Even in inscriptions that we would identify as "graffiti" today—the equivalent of "Carl was here"—the message emphasizes the act of carving the runes. For example, one anonymous inscription found in the Orkney Islands reads, "These runes were carved by the man most skilled in runes in the western ocean." Another, on a church in Norway, reads "Thorir carved these runes on the eve of Olaus-mass, when he travelled past here. The norns did both good and evil, great toil... they created for me."

As we can see, the runes were an integral part of the culture of ancient Northern Europe and held great symbolic as well as magical power. We will soon delve into the use of runes in magic and divination today, but first, let's take a moment to get better acquainted with the specific symbols we'll be working with in this guide.

THE ELDER FUTHARK

Generally, when speaking of "the runes," we may be referring to one or more of several different runic scripts (aka alphabets) known today. Unlike our English alphabet, there is no single, standardized set of characters that make up a universal runic script.

This is because as the Germanic peoples continued to spread out into new territories in western and central Europe, the language that the first runes represented—known as "Proto-Germanic"—eventually split into regional dialects. As these dialects became more and more distinct from the original Proto-Germanic, the first runic script, known today as the Elder Futhark, was adapted to meet the needs of the newly evolving languages. Among various runic scripts, runes were added to represent new sounds coming into the languages, existing sounds were represented by new runic symbols, and some runes were omitted altogether.

It's unclear exactly how many different runic scripts existed within the Germanic lands over the centuries, but two distinct descendants of the Elder Futhark came into wide use between the 5th and 12th centuries C.E.. The Anglo-Saxon Futhorc was developed in Frisia (now Denmark and part of Germany) and spread to England with the migrations of Germanic tribes. The Younger Futhark came to replace the Elder in Scandinavia by the eighth century, and this is the script used during the Viking Age.

Today's Neopagans, magicians and other rune workers may use runes from one of these systems exclusively, or more than one, depending on their practice. Many also incorporate lesser-known runic scripts, such as the Gothic and Medieval runes, or the Armanen runes discussed above. Among those who practice Witchcraft, there is also a modern set of "Witch's runes," which are inspired by the ancient runes but bear very little resemblance to any of the authentic runic scripts.

For the sake of simplicity, this guide will focus only on the runes of the Elder Futhark, as these are, after all, the "original" runes. They are also the most widely available when it comes to purchasing a pre-made set of runes. This doesn't mean that the Younger Futhark and the Anglo-Saxon Futhorc are not equally powerful and worthy of study. You may ultimately wish to work with one of these systems, or with Gothic or Armanen runes. If so, the information in this guide will still provide a valuable place to begin your runic explorations.

The Elder Futhark (pronounced "footh-ark"), and named for the first six runes in the script, is comprised of 24 symbols, each representing a sound in the Proto-Germanic language. But a closer look at the structure and makeup of the Elder Futhark uncovers the magical essence of the runes as they have always been, well before their evolution into a written script:

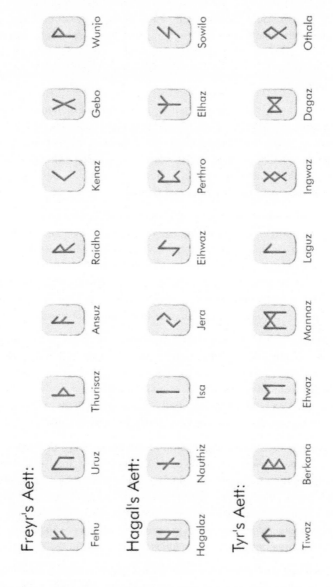

Freyr's Aett:

Fehu — Uruz — Thurisaz — Ansuz — Raidho — Kenaz — Gebo — Wunjo

Hagal's Aett:

Hagalaz — Nauthiz — Isa — Jera — Eihwaz — Perthro — Elhaz — Sowilo

Tyr's Aett:

Tiwaz — Berkana — Ehwaz — Mannaz — Laguz — Ingwaz — Dagaz — Othala

First, the names of the characters have actual meanings, such as "gift" (Gebo), "Sun" (Sowilo), and "water" (Laguz). By contrast, the names of the letters in most other European-based alphabets have no meaning. (The two other exceptions are Hebrew and the ancient Irish alphabet known as Ogham, both of which were also utilized for esoteric purposes.)

The names of the runes come from the everyday experience of the people who used them. Objects such as cattle, torches, horses, and trees are represented among the runes, as are natural phenomena like water, ice, and the Sun. Intangible experiences, such as strength, need, and joy, along with divine forces, including the gods Tyr and Ing, are also incorporated into the system of symbols.

But these names are not necessarily literal when applied in divination and other forms of magic—most of the time, the meanings associated with the runes are rooted in metaphors and esoteric associations. For example, drawing Ehwaz ("horse") is not likely in most cases to refer to an actual horse. Instead, Ehwaz symbolizes the qualities of faithfulness and trust, which a relationship between a horse and its rider requires. It can also refer to movement or travel.

Dagaz ("dawn") is not so much about the time of day, but instead represents breakthrough, transformation, and hope. In this way each rune name serves as a bridge between the human mind and the ethereal realm of divine wisdom that the runes inhabit. In contemplating both the symbol itself and the implications of its name, we come to an understanding of the energies of each rune.

Second, the Elder Futhark is divided into three groups of eight runes, known collectively as the aettir (Old Norse for "families"). The origins of this organization are unclear, and many artifacts bearing an inscription of the full Elder Futhark present the runes in one horizontal row, rather than three rows of eight. But other inscriptions show the above configuration, and much esoteric meaning has been derived from the three aettir over the centuries.

Each aett (or "family") is named for the god who is associated with the first rune in the row. The first row, beginning with Fehu, is known as Freyr's Aett (sometimes called "Frey's Aett"). The second row, beginning with Hagalaz, is Hagal's Aett, though since little is known about the god Hagal, some people attribute this aett to Heimdall. Tyr's Aett, beginning with Teiwaz, makes up the third row.

These divisions make it easier to learn and memorize the names and shapes of the runes, but they also create patterns of relationships among the runes that can be useful in magic. For example, we can look at possible connections between Uruz, Naudiz, and Berkana—the second runes in each aett.

Uruz is the rune of brute strength, while Naudiz represents strong need. Berkana is known as the birth rune, on literal and figurative levels. Anyone familiar with childbirth knows that strength is needed for a successful delivery, but this combination can also speak to a need giving rise to the birth of a new idea that lends great strength to a project or enterprise. These relationships between the runes can add meaning and context to rune readings and truly enhance magical work.

Mystical students of the runes have also noted that each of these rune "families" have their own collective associations, based on the meanings of each rune. These associations vary from one runic tradition to the next, but can be generally characterized as follows: Freyr's Aett symbolizes the forces of creation, Hagal's Aett is concerned with forces of disruption and change, and Tyr's Aett represents divine forces as they relate to the human experience. Furthermore, the progressive order of the runes is significant, as runes within each row are seen to have interactive symbolic relationships with runes before and/or after them.

This level of complexity in runic interpretation goes beyond the scope of this beginner's guide. However, as you become more acquainted and practiced with the runes, you will no doubt begin to sense the connections between individual runes based on their placement within the Elder Futhark.

In some respects, the runes can be said to have similarities to the systems of symbology within the Tarot. The four suits of the Minor Arcana seem to echo the thematic organization of the three aettir, while the deliberate ordering of the cards in the Major Arcana recalls the overall structure and resulting symbolic relationships of the Elder Futhark.

In fact, some have theorized that the Tarot was inspired at least in part by the runes, and comparisons and even correspondences between specific runes and specific cards have been made. However, these possible relationships are also beyond the scope of this guide. In truth, while they can be useful for those who have experience in Tarot, comparisons between the two systems can actually distract from learning the runes on their own terms.

MAGIC AND TRADITION

Now that we've seen how the symbols known as runes came into use as a system for writing, as well as their magical significance in Norse myth, we're ready to explore their uses in modern magic and divination. In Part Two, you'll be introduced to the basics of working with rune magic—from making your own runes, to harnessing their energy in spellwork, to receiving communications from the unseen world through runic symbols. But before we move forward, it's important to address the extent to which the information in the following pages is directly connected to the practices of ancient Germanic runemasters.

Much of contemporary "Western" magic practiced by Wiccans and other Neopagans today can be described as a synthesis of pan-European influences. Threads of Hermeticism, Neoplatonism, ceremonial magic, and other elements of what is often called the Western Mystery Tradition, along with various folk traditions from around the globe and countless intuitive innovations, have been interwoven to create highly individualized magical systems among today's eclectic practitioners.

The sources from which these blends of modern magic have been created can range from ancient Egyptian texts, classical grimoires, and anthropological evidence to family traditions and divinely-inspired discoveries. The magical tools and materials involved also vary widely and may include ceremonial wands, bottles and pins, crystals and herbs, and many other items. In short, much of the magic you learn about today is a heterogenous mishmash of practices with no clear, traceable roots to one specific region of the world.

By comparison, those who work with rune magic are drawing specifically on what is known about the magical traditions of the pre-

Christian Germanic peoples— the people from whom the runes have been handed down over time. Much of this information comes from the mythology, literature, and lore of ancient Scandinavia, but clues can also be found in fragments of myth from other parts of the Germanic world, as well as historical texts, archeological findings, and other scholarly pursuits.

Of course, there is not enough information to reconstruct a completely accurate picture of what rune magic entailed in prior centuries, so here, too, intuition plays a role in creating modern practices. However, the degree of borrowing and synthesizing beliefs and practices from other cultures, as we see in more "mainstream" magic, is far less prevalent among most rune workers, who prefer to root their practice firmly within the Germanic tradition.

This doesn't mean that the runes can only be utilized by those who practice Germanic magic. The energies of these symbols are universal and can be harnessed by anyone who is willing to learn, regardless of religious or spiritual path.

The magical workings in this guide are intended to be accessible to those who are not familiar with the lore and cosmology of the cultures from which the runes originated, and should not be viewed as historically authentic. Yet they do draw on a basic understanding of traditional rune magic, and can serve as a jumping-off point for those who would like to learn more about Germanic beliefs and magical practices. So with both an eclectic spirit and an appreciation for tradition, let's look now at how you can utilize the energies of these ancient symbols for magic in your daily life.

PART TWO

RUNES IN MAGIC AND DIVINATION

GETTING ACQUAINTED WITH THE RUNES

As we saw in Part One, the runes represent various aspects—both tangible and intangible— of the Universe as it is experienced by human beings. When it comes to magic, we take this concept deeper: each runic symbol embodies a natural force, or type of energy, which the rune worker can attune to and then work with in various ways.

The energies of the runes are utilized to send magical "instructions" for manifestation, and to receive messages from the spiritual realm. In this sense, the runes are fairly simple to work with, and you can form an affinity with one or a handful of runes to use in talismans or other spellwork without much further exploration. However, the full range of magical possibilities and divinatory meanings of all the runes is only grasped through dedicated study and practice.

As mentioned earlier, a background in Norse mythology and/or Germanic magic is not necessary for successful rune work, but any knowledge you acquire in these areas will certainly help. At the very least, a cursory introduction to the main Norse myths and deities can assist you with forging some basic connections with these symbols. You'll find some suggested resources in the recommended reading list at the end of this guide.

Of course, no amount of book learning can substitute for experience, so it's important to give yourself time to practice as well, particularly when you're just beginning to learn the names and meanings of the runes. One approach that works well is to study and meditate on one rune per day, for 24 days, which allows you to focus solely on that particular symbol's energies without getting distracted by any of the other runes.

Carry the day's rune with you in your pocket or purse, keep it visible whenever possible, and keep it by your bedside while you sleep. You can work through the Elder Futhark from beginning to end, or choose a rune intuitively each morning until you've spent one day with each of them.

As you learn about each rune's magical significance and divinatory meanings, be sure to incorporate your own intuition as well. The intellectual understanding of the symbol is one thing, but your psychic connection with each rune will ultimately override any information you get from an outside source.

Try simply gazing at each symbol and listening to any feelings, words or other impressions that come through. Some runes may "give up" more information than others during this process. Don't worry if there are runes that don't seem to want to communicate with you just yet—all of this takes time. After all, even Odin the "Allfather" had to wait nine days and nights to grasp the runes, while hanging upside down from a tree!

As you begin to train your focus on the shapes of the runes, you may start to see them appear in your surroundings—in shadows made by tree branches, cracks in sidewalks, or even in cloud formations. This is a good sign that you are attuning to runic energies, and that the Universe is offering you a new avenue of divine communication. The more you work with the runes, the more you will be able to tap into these energies and call upon them in your magic. The core elements of runic magic and divination below will provide you with an excellent place to start.

41

RUNE MAGIC:
THE POWER OF SOUND,
SPEECH, AND SYMBOL

Symbols have always been a part of magical systems throughout the world. They can be thought of as a tool for communicating visually, rather than verbally, with the Universe.

Symbols help us express complex ideas in relatively simple forms that work on the invisible planes of reality to manifest our desires. In Germanic lore, runic symbols were used for a wide range of magical purposes, even before they came to be part of a written script. However, once the runes were incorporated into a writing system, they became even more magically potent.

This is because the Germanic peoples placed great value on the power of the spoken word. Speaking a thought out loud was to make the thought real in a way that could never be reversed. Careless speech could therefore have serious consequences, no matter how unintentional. This is still true today, of course, but in modern times we can often negate the impact of our words by apologizing or clarifying our meaning. In the past, once a word or phrase was uttered, it remained part of the world no matter what.

Because the runes provided a way for words to be communicated over time and distance in a previously non-literate society, they were incredibly powerful indeed. Now the magical power of symbol was fused with the power of speech, which is also intertwined with the power of sound, in the form of magical vibrations created within the body. Today's rune workers often speak, chant, or sing the names of the runes as part of their magical practice, as we will see below.

USING RUNES IN MODERN MAGIC

Those who choose to learn rune magic in the context of traditional Germanic practices are likely to come across differences between the ancient Northern European worldview and our own. For one thing, the runemasters in Norse mythology wouldn't bat an eye at what Wiccans and other Neopagans might term "black" or "negative" magic. Rune spells for manipulating people and causing harm to enemies were plentiful and considered essential in many circumstances. This guide, however, promotes the modern magical ethic of "harm none."

Secondly, there is the question of whether using the wrong runes by mistake will have negative or otherwise unintended consequences, such as in the story of Egill and the sick woman mentioned in Part One. Unintended consequences are possible in any kind of magic, which is why it's always advisable to put deep thought into how to communicate your desires to the Universe. However, in the case of using the "wrong" runes, it's more likely that your magic will be ineffective, as opposed to harmful. What matters most is the quality of your focused intention during the work. As with any other magical tool, your personal energy must be present to activate the powers of any rune.

Norse literature also shows us that the runemasters of old recognized different categories of runes, according to how they were used. For example, *malrunes* were useful in matters relating to words and language, while *hugrunes* were concerned with mental ability. *Brunrunes* were for ensuring good weather at sea, which was obviously crucial during the Viking era, and *limrunes* were used in healing the sick.

Today's rune workers may differ in their individual understandings of any given rune's magical purposes (just as differences emerge within correspondence systems for herbs, crystals, and colors), but a general consensus based on the lore and literature of the Germanic tribes has been established for well over a century. You'll find the chief magical uses for each rune in Part Three and in the tables of correspondence at the end of this guide. These can serve as a framework for your rune magic, but if you arrive at different conclusions about the appropriate use for any rune, then make adjustments according to your own intuition and experience.

RUNIC INSCRIPTIONS

The most widely practiced form of rune magic today is the use of runes in magical inscriptions. Traditionally, runes are carved into objects to create talismans for luck and protection. These can be personal objects, such as jewelry, drinking cups, wallets, or even houses— anything of value that you want to empower or protect with magical energy.

Runic talismans can also be created to achieve a specific magical goal, such as landing a job or attracting a new love relationship. In this case, the runes are carved into a 'tine," which is usually a strip of wood or bark, but can also be stone, metal, or even paper if need be. Carving is the traditional method, but runes can also be drawn and/or painted onto a surface to make a talisman, provided that sufficient care and concentration goes into creating the runic shapes.

As with any magical creation, the energy involved in the process of making the talisman is key to its success. In fact, rune workers often incorporate the creation of a talisman into a ritual, which involves the carving and coloring of the runes, the speaking or singing of the names of the runes being used, and a symbolic "birthing" and consecration of the talismanic object.

Runic talismans, like the runes themselves, are considered to be "alive" with magical energy. They are either kept permanently, or, in the case of rune tines, they are ritually "released" from existence once their magical purpose has been fulfilled, often by burning or burying them in the Earth.

RUNE SCRIPTS

The simplest form of magical runic inscription is a series of runes carved in a horizontal row. The runes and the order they appear in are chosen deliberately according to the magical goal.

Typically, a rune script will have at least 3 and generally not more than 9 runes. Rune workers rooted in Germanic traditional magic usually choose an odd number—either 3, 5, 7, or 9—but there's no reason to avoid using even numbers if they resonate with you.

The most important factor is that you've considered the meanings and magical uses of the chosen runes carefully, and placed them in the order that best represents your magical goal. Think of the rune script as "telling the story" of what you want the outcome to be. And keep in mind that more runes doesn't necessarily equal a more powerful talisman. If you load it up with more than you need to communicate your intentions effectively, you run the risk of energetically "cluttering" the work.

A TRAVELING TALISMAN

As an example, you can create a talisman for safe travels by using the following runes in a rune script: Raidho (riding); Uruz (strength); Ehwaz (horse); Kenaz (beacon).

The basic "story" of this talisman is one of traveling with strength and good health along a well-lighted path. Both Raidho and Ehwaz are used in magic for safe travels, while Uruz, placed between them, is a rune of strength and healing. Kenaz represents light, warmth, and illumination, and is also used as a general strengthening agent in many rune scripts.

In the above ordering, the forward-pointing shape of Kenaz is emphasized, evoking forward, illuminated movement for the traveler. However, you could also place Kenaz between Raidho and Ehwaz, for more symmetry based on the runes' magical uses. Or, you might decide not to include Kenaz, and/or to switch out Uruz for a rune representing some other aspect of your travel that's important to you. Keeping both Raidho and Ehwaz makes sense, since they both relate to travel, but perhaps there's another rune that's even more relevant to your particular journey.

The rationale for four runes in this particular example is that the number four represents stability, which can be a desirable quality when traveling. However, you can certainly remove a rune or add another appropriate rune for an odd-numbered version, if that resonates more with you.

This can be one of the most rewarding parts of the whole process— simply exploring and considering the implications of the runes you incorporate into your talisman. As you do so, you hone in on your intentions for the work, and strengthen your magical focus to see it through. This is why it's not really advisable to find and use pre-written rune scripts for a given magical purpose (although you are of course free to use the above example). If you don't create the script yourself, you're not participating in the envisioning process as deeply.

BIND RUNES

A related form of runic inscription is called a bind rune—two or more runes that are superimposed on each other in an aesthetically pleasing way. Instead of appearing as distinct, individual magical forces in a linear arrangement, the runes in a bind rune form a single symbol that blends and amplifies their combined magical energies.

⋈ Dagaz

↑ Tiwaz x2

ᚲ Perthro x2

For example, this bind rune combines three runes used in healing magic. The center rune is Dagaz, flanked on either side by Perthro. A double version of Tiwaz runs vertically through the center of Dagaz. This image can be inscribed on a candle, drawn on paper, painted onto a canvas to hang on the wall, or used in a traditional runic talisman as described below. After superimposing the runes together, this is the end result:

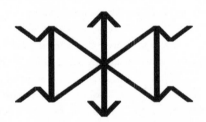

Depending on your artistic abilities, bind runes may be more complex to create than rune scripts, but attempting them is a great way to further familiarize yourself with the runes and their individual energies. Bind runes also work well when you want to keep a magical working "hidden in plain sight," such as when turning a personal object into a talisman. To the uninitiated, a bind rune will usually just look like an interesting design.

As with rune scripts, you should carefully consider and select the runes you incorporate into the bind rune. It's advisable to stick with just two to three runes when you're just beginning, so you get a good feel for how they interact with each other, both visually and energetically. Just as with rune scripts, too many runes can easily get counterproductive, and in this case can make it hard to recognize the individual runes within the design.

As for placement, this is often dictated by what will make the most harmonious design, but a good rule of thumb is to make sure that the central rune is associated with your overall magical goal. For example, if you're making a fertility charm, placing Berkana, Jera, or Ingwaz at the center of the bind rune is a good place to start.

The runes in a bind rune can be backwards, sideways, upside-down, or at any angle—there's no need to worry about keeping them in an "upright" position in order to avoid sending "reversed rune" energy into the Universe. You can also repeat a rune more than once within the design, as shown above. This is part of the fun of bind runes—you can get very visually playful. And as you gain more experience, you will likely notice a rune or two in your designs that you didn't even intend to include!

CREATING A RUNIC TALISMAN

The instructions below are for creating a single-purpose magical talisman, to be used for a specific aim and then released. If you want to transform a permanent object into a talisman, simply modify the instructions as appropriate, according to the sturdiness and material makeup of the object.

As mentioned above, the making of the talisman is often done as part of a ritual, so feel free to begin the process in whatever way you would normally start a ritual, whether that involves casting a circle, invoking your personal deities, or simply lighting a few candles. We'll cover the basic ritual of "birthing" and consecrating the talisman below, but here let's just focus on the nuts and bolts.

Materials

For a traditional runic talisman, you'll need a "tine" to carve the runes into, a carving tool, pigment(s) for coloring the runes after they're carved, a cloth for wrapping the talisman, and a cord or string, preferably made of natural materials, to wrap around the talisman nine times.

The tine can be any naturally-derived material. If using wood, consider aligning the type of tree with the magical purpose at hand. (The same goes for metals and even mineral stones.) In some traditions, the tine is made from a branch harvested from a live tree.

This can be an ethically sticky subject, as some Neopagans would argue that a living plant should never be harmed unless it's absolutely necessary, and it's just as effective to use a fallen branch instead. However, those who do use a live branch believe they are keeping with ancient traditions, and are careful to secure permission from the tree, and leave it offerings to thank it for its sacrifice. How you choose to acquire the wood for your tine is up to you, but cutting a branch from a live tree with carelessness is not recommended.

Traditionally, the carved runes are colored with blood and/or natural pigments made from rocks and soil. (This is up to you, but don't ever feel the need to cause yourself pain in order to work magic. After all, there are some practices our ancestors engaged in that we have left behind in modern times, for good reason.) You can find instructions on making your own pigments online, but you can also use watercolor or acrylic paint if you like. (Oil-based paints are not recommended.)

The runemasters of old used red in order to empower the carved runes, but contemporary rune workers have incorporated various color systems to expand the possibilities for magical associations. Any color can be used, but using shades of red, green, or blue is a nice way to keep within the spirit of the old Norse culture, as these were the three colors recognized in those days.

Speaking of magical associations, there are other opportunities to enrich the work, such as using numerology and timing. Various systems of numerology have been integrated into rune magic, using the number assigned to each rune according to its placement in the Futhark. If you incorporate numerology into your practice, this can be an extra consideration in your selection of runes for your talisman.

As for timing, the usual magical guidelines apply: talismans for increase or attraction are best made during the waxing Moon, while those for banishing or decrease are most powerful when made during the waning Moon. Some rune workers also take correspondences related to the season, the day of the week, and even the hour of the day into consideration.

Process

To begin, turn the tine over and carve the name of the person the talisman is for (usually you, unless you're making it for someone else, with their permission). Use runic letters for the name—you'll find a conversion chart for English letters at the end of this guide. Then carve the rune script or bind rune on the front of the tine. (As mentioned above, if you're not comfortable with carving, you can draw the runes instead.) Be as artful as you can, taking care with your craftsmanship to create an aesthetically pleasing talisman.

Next, apply the color to the runes on the back and front of the tine. As you do so, speak, chant, or sing the name of each rune, and visualize it infusing the tine with its magical energies according to your goal. Your focus throughout the process should be on your intention, and the summoning of the runic forces to aid you in your manifestation. As you work, the energies of the runes are combining to form your specific request to the Universe.

ACTIVATING YOUR TALISMAN

When the pigment is dry, you're ready to ritually activate the magical power of the talisman. This ritual can range from simple to highly elaborate, depending on your personal approach. All ritual exists to aid the magician's focus and connection with the unseen energies of the natural world, so do what works for you in your practice. You may wish to cast a magic circle, invoke any deities you work with (Norse deities would be particularly appropriate here), use candles, burn incense, etc. Here we will just lay out the bare bones of a traditional runic talisman ritual:

- Quiet your mind and spend some time visualizing your magical goal.

- Wrap the talisman in the cloth, and wrap the cord around it nine times. It's traditional to leave magically-charged runes in "darkness" for a period while its power grows, symbolizing a new life developing in the womb.

- Lay the wrapped talisman on your altar or work space and walk around it in a sunwise (clockwise) circle 9 times. Alternatively, you can carry it with you. As you walk, speak the names of the runes in the talisman, and/or of the magical outcome you seek.

- Unwrap the talisman, and breathe on it to give it life. You may wish to also give it a magical name.

- Consecrate the talisman by waving it quickly through a candle flame, sprinkling it with water and salt, and/or passing it through incense smoke.

- State the talisman's purpose a final time. It is now activated and ready to work its magic. Depending on its size and purpose, you can leave it in a place where you'll see it often, carry it with you, or hide it.

- Close the ritual in whatever way is appropriate to your practice.

- When the magical goal has manifested, release the talisman by burning it or burying it in the Earth.

OTHER FORMS
OF RUNE MAGIC

Talismans are a staple of rune magic, but other traditional practices from the ancient Germanic world have also been revived by modern rune workers.

Stadhagaldr, also known as "runic yoga," involves the use of the body to create runic shapes, thereby physically embodying the energy of the runes. Another physical form is *galdr*, or sacred singing, which utilizes the magic of sound and speech and can be performed on its own or incorporated into other work such as the talisman ritual above. Runes are also used in sign magic, in which the rune worker makes the sign of a rune with their hand, finger, or wand. This may be part of a ritual, or used to invoke protection in various circumstances.

Outside of the context of Germanic magic, runes are also used in candle spells, worn around the neck as talismans, traced in soil, sand, and bodies of water in nature magic, and used as a magical alphabet for encoding a Book of Shadows. Truthfully, the topic of rune magic as a whole is vast and beyond the scope of this introductory guide, but you'll find plenty of more in-depth resources to explore on the recommended reading page.

RUNIC DIVINATION

Before you begin using the runes in divination, it's important to understand that what runic readings present is not a prediction of unalterable fate. Rather, successful divination of any kind provides what could be called a "snapshot" of the present moment, which can illuminate unseen factors in your situation and point to probable outcomes based on your current course of action.

Remember that in the worldview of the ancient Norse, the future is always shifting according to what is happening in the present. The messages of the runes are meant to be empowering navigational tools, as once you have a clear picture of your circumstances, you can make informed choices about how to proceed. It's also important to remember that, ultimately, you are your best source of wisdom. Use the runes as guides, but don't override your own intuitively-based decision making abilities because of a rune reading.

Furthermore, don't allow an over-reliance on the runes to weaken your natural powers of discernment. If you find yourself automatically turning to the runes whenever you have to make a decision about anything at all, then you're likely suffering from "oracle abuse." It's far better to save the runes for truly important questions that you can't find an answer for on your own.

YOUR OWN SET OF RUNES

Although the use of runes in magical workings does not require an actual set of runes, having physical representations of each runic character is still helpful for connecting with their energies, and is of course necessary for divination. Traditionally, rune sets are hand-made by the person who will use them, which imbues the symbols with the unique energetic signature of the rune worker for a truly one-of-a-kind divination tool.

To make your own set of runes, you can follow the basic processes described above for making talismans. As with traditional runic talismans, the materials you make your runes from should be natural—either wood, bone, stone, or clay. If you're not equipped for wood or stone cutting, you could work with pre-cut wood chips, or collect small, flat rocks or pebbles.

If you're basing your set on the Elder Futhark, you will need 24 individual pieces. It's best to use roughly the same size and shape so that you won't be able to tell them apart when they're face-down. Also, avoid any identifying marks on the backs of your runes for the same reason.

You can find plenty of different approaches to rune-making online, often with detailed instructions for cutting, carving, painting, and sealing or polishing your runes to help keep their symbols bright and visible over time.

If making your own runes isn't feasible, however, you can find pre-made rune sets in many different varieties. Some sets consist of small clay tablets carved with runic symbols, while others use tumbled mineral stones or pieces of wood or metal. (Depending on how you want to approach divination, tumbled mineral stones may not be very practical, since they may not have flat enough surfaces to easily distinguish the runes that land "face up.")

If buying runes doesn't appeal to you either, you can easily make rune cards instead, which offers the opportunity to practice drawing the symbols, and can help in the process of familiarizing yourself with the runes and their meanings. You can even use rune cards for divination, though it will obviously be more akin to reading Tarot than to traditional runic divination. The rune spreads described below can be used with either rune cards or rune sets.

No matter where your runes originate or the material they're made from, be sure to do a clearing and consecration ritual before using them in divination. For example, use smudging herbs like sage or rosemary, leave the runes out overnight in moonlight, or place them in a bowl of earth or salt (depending on the material) overnight to clear them of unwanted energy. Then send out your intention for these symbols to serve as your connecting bridge to the divine, in whichever way is most appropriate for your personal practice.

Carry your runes with you and keep them near you for at least three days to strengthen your energetic connection to them. Treat them with an animistic perspective—see them as living beings that can assist you in a multitude of ways, as long as they are well cared for.

Runes are traditionally stored in a cloth pouch, which may or may not be included with a store-bought rune set. You can often find quality draw-string bags in magical supply shops or online, or you can make your own if you're handy with a needle and thread.

For divination, you'll also want to have a rune cloth for casting the runes upon, or as a designated space for laying out rune spreads. The traditional color for the rune cloth is white, but the more important factor is that it's a plain cloth with no visual distractions to pull your focus from the rune cast. A typical rune cloth is 18 by 18 inches, but depending on your preference and the size of your runes, you may opt for something larger or smaller.

TIPS FOR SUCCESSFUL DIVINATION

For the clearest reading possible, you'll need a calm, quiet place to work in and a clear mind. Don't be casting runes with the television on, or right after you've had an upsetting or frustrating experience. Take the time to meditate for a few moments, breathing deeply, and then think about your question.

As the querent (or the person asking the question), you are the conduit through which the runes communicate. If your own energy is "cloudy" due to anxiety or extraneous thoughts, then you will likely get a cloudy reading.

Asking the Right Questions

So what kinds of questions can the runes help you answer? There's really no limit to what you can ask in terms of subject matter—whether it's related to relationships, careers, health issues, or anything else important to you, the runes can provide good counsel.

Although some people do use runes to answer "yes or no" questions, with upright runes standing for yes and reversed for no, this type of question is often not well suited for runic divination. For example, asking "should I buy this house?" is unlikely to result in a clear or satisfying reading.

Instead, you could ask what the outcome of buying the house looks like, given your present circumstances. Then, in a new rune cast, you might ask about the outcome of passing on this particular opportunity. Approaching the issue from this less direct approach allows for more potential information to come through than simply asking for a "yes or no" answer.

Reversed Runes

Of the 24 runes in the Elder Futhark, nine of them look essentially the same whether they are upright or upside down ("reversed"). These symbols have the same meanings no matter which way they appear in the rune cast. The rest of the runes are interpreted differently depending on whether they are upright or reversed after you turn them over.

Often, the reversed interpretation of a rune is the inverse or "opposite" of its upright meaning, but this is not always the case—it may just indicate a different angle on the subject than the upright meaning would indicate. Some people fear reversed runes, perceiving them as portending "bad news," and there are even rune readers who don't recognize reversed interpretations at all.

Your approach to reversed runes is entirely up to you, but if you want to get the most out of what these symbols have to offer, then try considering reversed runes as useful signals. A reversed rune can be like a traffic light, letting you know whether it's safe to proceed, or whether you should wait awhile before moving forward.

Runic Combinations

Generally speaking, each rune in a reading has its own message for you, but their meanings can also play off of each other to provide even more specific information about your question.

There are recognized combinations of two runes and three runes that can be interpreted in certain ways to clarify or add new layers to the reading. For example, if you draw Fehu (wealth) along with Raidho (travel), then you may be about to gain something valuable in connection with a journey. If Nauthiz (need) accompanies Fehu, the wealth you gain may be coming in to resolve a specific financial problem.

These combinations and their associated meanings are not learned overnight, and they can vary widely from reader to reader, depending on one's personal understanding of each rune. You will develop your own sense for rune pairs and rune trios as you gain experience.

For now, just focus on individual meanings first, and then begin to look at how the runes may be working together on an additional level. You may want to keep track of your readings in a notebook or journal as you go, to measure their accuracy and record any insights that arise.

Repeating Runes and Runic Override

As you begin to get more experience in reading the runes, you may notice over time that the same rune or pair of runes keeps turning up in your readings. If this is the case, pay extra close attention to their meanings, as you are being guided to look at an important aspect of your approach to a situation, or to your life in general.

Another way the runes may guide you with extra emphasis is by speaking about something entirely unrelated to your question. If this happens, don't automatically dismiss the reading as a "dud." Instead, explore what the rune(s) in question may be pointing to, as there could be other, more pressing matters that need your attention.

Preparing the Reading

Rune readers working in the context of the Germanic tradition will cast the runes onto the rune cloth, as mentioned above. Some people have a ritual for unfolding the cloth and spreading it on the ground or table where the reading is taking place. They might also align themselves and the cloth with a specific direction, usually to the north or the east. On the other hand, other readers might not even use a rune cloth at all. As with so much about magic in general, this is also entirely up to you.

When it comes to "shuffling," the runes in order to cast them at random, there are a few different approaches you might take. You can simply scramble them around in the rune pouch and then take out the number of runes you'll be reading. Or you can lay them all out face-down and swirl them around with your fingers. If your runes are small enough that all of them will fit in your cupped palms, you can mix them around that way. Try a few different methods to discover which works best for you.

TRADITIONAL RUNE CASTING

As we saw in Part One, what we know of the traditional methods of runic divination comes from the Roman writer Tacitus, who described the practice nearly 2,000 years ago in his book *Germania*. Many rune readers prefer to follow this method today, not just because of its connection to our pagan ancestors, but because it facilitates an interaction with the runes that is more free-associative than the more "prescriptive" rune spreads of the modern era.

Depending on your approach, you may choose to incorporate a number of elements into your interpretation, such as any patterns or shapes created by runes as they land, the combinations of runes that fall close to each other, the distance from any given rune to your body, or to the edge of the rune cloth, etc. For people whose psychic talents favor the visual senses, traditional rune casting is particularly useful, but it's a good exercise for anyone seeking to forge an intuitive connection to the runes.

To work as closely with ancient tradition as possible, you will need to cut a new set of runes from the branch of a fruit-bearing tree, being sure to ask the tree's permission and giving thanks for its sacrifice. The advantage to this step is that the runes are "fresh," created solely for the purpose of this reading, and thus imbued with a special energy. However, if you're not comfortable taking a living tree branch, you can work with runes drawn on small stones, or simply use your existing set of runes. (You may want to smudge or otherwise ritually clear them of past energies before beginning the rune cast). If possible, perform this divination outdoors for an even closer connection with the energies of the runes.

When you're ready to cast, "shuffle" the runes and gently scatter them onto the rune cloth. Be sure to look upward so that you don't see any of the runes as they land. Keeping your gaze upward, choose three runes at random, picking them up one at a time. Read the runes both separately, considering their meanings individually, and then consider the implications of the three of them together.

You may choose to note the direction they appeared in when you picked them up and read any reverse meanings, or you may just focus on the overall theme(s) of the runes as important elements to focus on at this time. You can also read the three runes as aspects of your past, present, and future, according to the order in which you picked them up.

This method, as described Tacitus, can be adapted in countless ways. For example, you can vary the number of runes you choose to pick up at random. Or you can read all of the runes that land upright, although, depending on how many do, you may end up with more symbols to interpret than are useful to deriving real meaning from the reading. In this event, you can look for significances among combinations of runes, as discussed above, as well as visual patterns and shapes in the overall arrangement of the runes.

Another variation is to take a handful of small twigs and cast them onto the cloth, and identify runic symbols that are organically created by the shapes in which the twigs land. This style of reading is a wonderful way to work directly with Nature, and also helps you hone your overall attunement to runic shapes in the outer world.

RUNE SPREADS

Unlike traditional rune casting, rune spreads are a modern innovation, much more akin to the Tarot of the Western Mystery Tradition than to older forms of Northern European magic.

However, certain aspects of rune spreads are rooted in the Germanic worldview, such as an emphasis on odd numbers. The most commonly used spreads use one, three, five, seven, or nine runes. (Both three and nine are particularly important numbers in Norse cosmology.)

Each of these spreads can have several versions, with different meanings for each position in the spread, depending on the facets of the situation one wishes to learn about. For example, one version of a five rune spread might focus on a linear timeline of events surrounding the question, while another may reveal aspects of the people, challenges, and/or hidden factors involved.

ONE RUNE

Sometimes called "Odin's Rune," this method is rather self-explanatory: shuffle the runes around in their pouch and pull out one rune. This is an effective approach when you want some advice about a decision you need to make quickly or an unexpected situation you need to respond to.

It can also serve as a small ritual for self-reflection as you start your day. What theme(s) does the rune bring up that would be beneficial to meditate on at this time?

You might even carry your selected rune with you throughout your day as an anchoring point to return to if you start to get overly caught up in trivial details at work, school, or social events. In this way, the runes help you stay in tune with your magical inner self amid the hustle and bustle of modern life.

THREE RUNES

Past   Present   Future

The three runes method provides more context than one rune, but still paints in fairly broad strokes when it comes to seeing the full scope of a situation. The runes are laid out side by side and are read from left to right. The classic three rune spread, a number evocative of the Norns, reflects past, present, and future developments related to your question.

For example, in this reading, the querent has asked about the possibilities for finding a new love relationship:

Past   Present   Future
Kenaz   Ehwaz   Ingwaz
(Reversed)

The rune in the past position, Kenaz reversed, suggests that a relationship has recently ended, leaving the querent feeling abandoned and possibly confused about what went wrong. Ehwaz in the present position indicates that the querent is learning much-needed lessons about faith and trust, whether in the context of relationships or simply in the process of the querent's own personal journey. Ehwaz also suggests that swift change may be taking place.

Ingwaz, a very positive rune in general, is a great one to have in the future position. It indicates that a healthy, hearty, passionate relationship is on its way! The querent can rest assured that the loss suffered in the past is not the end of the story, and that whatever the challenges of the present may be, they are preparing the querent for future gains.

When casting a three rune reading, the order in which you lay down the runes depends on your preference and your concept of how the three positions relate to each other. Many people place the first rune in the past position and follow with present and future in linear fashion. Others see the present as the most important influence in the reading, and therefore place the first rune in the center, with the second in the past position and the third in the future.

A three rune spread can also be used for a "yes or no" question, with upright runes denoting yes and reversed denoting no. However, the actual symbols should still be read in their own right, since they provide context about the situation that can aid you in making the decision you're asking about. Or, if the answer is unclear, they can point to probabilities based on current circumstances.

Another three rune spread reveals aspects of a situation as it relates to your inner world and your response to it. This is particularly helpful when you're struggling with an unresolved issue or an unexpected development. It serves to clear emotional debris from your inner vision so you can view the situation with more objectivity.

The first rune, placed in the middle position, provides an objective overview. It answers the question, "What is at the heart of what's going on here?" The second rune is placed to the left and points to influences that led to this development, which are often hidden from the querent's view. The third rune, on the right, provides advice for adjusting your perspective, and may indicate a specific action you can take to best handle the current energies. This spread does not look into the future, as its main function is to center you objectively in the present.

FIVE RUNES

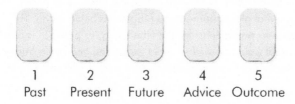

1	2	3	4	5
Past	Present	Future	Advice	Outcome

This five rune spread is an extension of the traditional three rune timeline of past (1), present (2), and future (3), but with a twist that emphasizes an aspect of the Norse concept of time: the continually-changing nature of the future based on present choices. The next rune offers advice regarding your question (4), in terms of how to act or how to reframe your perspective on the situation, knowing what you now know. The final rune then (5) speaks to the new or adjusted outcome that is most likely to arise if you follow the fourth rune's advice.

For example, in this reading, the querent wants to find a new place to live:

1	2	3	4	5
Mannaz	Isa	Eihwaz	Elhaz	Ansuz
(Reversed)			(Reversed)	

The rune in the past position reflects the approach the querent has been taking in this regard. Mannaz reversed suggests that the querent has been feeling negatively about the situation, perhaps due to comparisons between their current residence and perceived societal expectations of success. There has been a sense of misalignment between the querent's desires and their actual experience, which may actually have been clouding the querent's ability to approach the quest for housing with a clear head.

This interpretation is supported by Isa in the present position, indicating that at the moment, no progress is being made. The situation is frozen, at least for the time being, so patience is needed. The querent would do well to avoid expending energy on frustration about their current living situation, since it won't help move things along.

The good news is that Eihwaz in the future position points to a change, which will take place as a result of an old situation falling away. It looks like the querent will indeed find that new place to live, but this development will be experienced as a sense of regeneration after a period of dormant energy or even difficulty. The querent may encounter some other, unexpected change that contributes to a successful move. Keeping this rune in mind can help the querent avoid becoming anxious if any upheaval arises in the near future.

The rune in the advice position is Elhaz reversed. This is a strong rune of protection, which issues a warning when it appears reversed. The querent is advised to be on the lookout for seemingly good opportunities that they might regret taking, as someone—whether a real estate agent, a landlord, or a potential roommate—may be looking to take advantage of them. Although the querent's current dissatisfaction may make them eager to jump at the first new place that comes along, intuition is the most important factor at this time. If anything seems "off" about a housing offer, the querent should reject it and remain confident in an eventual positive outcome.

Assuming the querent heeds this advice, the outcome looks positive, with Ansuz in the final position. Ansuz represents messages and communication, which could come from people in the querent's life, new contacts, or even the spirit realm. This rune indicates that as long as the querent is patient, listens to intuition, and doesn't jump at the first opportunity to move simply in order to make a change, the right circumstances will fall into place. Better yet, when they do, the Universe will make it clear that the opportunity the querent has been waiting for is now available.

OTHER SPREADS

The above example is just one type of five rune spread. As with the three rune spread, many other possibilities exist, both for the physical arrangement of the runes and for the angles of the situation that the runes represent. You can find a wide array of these spreads online and in the suggested references at the end of this guide.

As for more detailed spreads, while it's true that more runes mean more information about your question, it's also fairly easy for a reading to get cloudy if too many runes are involved. Compared to Tarot readings, which frequently involve many cards, runic divination often tends to be an experience of "less is more." Perhaps this is because there are only 24 runes (give or take, depending on which runic alphabet you're working with), as opposed to the 78 cards in a standard Tarot deck. But it also seems to be just the nature of these symbols, especially for beginners, that too many in a spread can get overwhelming.

That's not to say that you shouldn't try spreads with six or more runes, but you may want to focus on the smaller spreads for awhile, as doing so will actually help you get to know the runes better. When you're ready to try more complex readings, you'll find plenty of possibilities out there (again, take a look at the recommended reading page at the end of this guide). Of course, you can always invent your own spreads as well!

MOVING FORWARD

When it comes to mastering the runes, the importance of time and practice can't be emphasized enough. As mentioned in Part One, there is always more to learn from the runes, even for the most adept rune workers. Hopefully the discussions above have provided you with a sufficient grounding to begin your runic practice with confidence. Now, it's time to meet the runes of the Elder Futhark.

In Part Three, you'll learn the names of the runes, their divinatory meanings, and their magical uses. These can serve as a broad foundation for your runic explorations, until you've developed your own personal understanding of the runes.

PART THREE
RUNE MEANINGS

RUNE INTERPRETATIONS AND MAGICAL USES

Before delving into the interpretations and magical uses of the runes, it's worth noting that the modern approach to runic divination and magic is likely quite different from that of the ancient Germanic pagans. The information below draws as much as possible from sources rooted in the traditions of these Northern European ancestors. However, even some of the earliest writing we have on the runes was influenced by non-native perspectives, including Christianity and even non-native magical belief systems such as Hermeticism and Gnosticism.

Among the sources that modern rune readers have relied on for historically-accurate information are three rune poems—the Old English Rune Poem (8th or 9th century), the Norwegian Rune Poem (13th century), and the Icelandic Rune Poem (15th century). Each of these works describes the runic script of its time and place, with stanzas that comment on some aspect of the name of each rune. Rune scholars have extrapolated many interpretations from these poems, along with many other primary sources such as the Norse mythology described in Part One.

A major forerunner of the modern divination approach was Guido von List (also mentioned in Part One), whose innovation of the Armanen runes was part of the Germanic Renaissance that revived much of the lore and religious traditions of the past. In fact, the Armanen runes were developed specifically for divination, rather than as a writing system. Yet even the work of List and other esoteric scholar-practitioners can't be guaranteed to be completely accurate when it comes to pre-Christian native practices.

Nonetheless, there's plenty of reason to believe that interpretations rooted in these scholarly efforts are as close to "the real thing" as we will ever get. And ultimately, the meanings of the runes are personal to each rune reader, so if a certain meaning comes to you through a given rune, then consider that to be its meaning, regardless of what you read in this or any other book. The same goes for magical uses—those listed here are considered to be part of the modern runic tradition, but you may find that your own relationship with any given rune is different.

There is one modern innovation to runic divination that you will likely come across in other sources but is not included in this guide: the "blank rune." Meant to represent the idea of fate, or destiny (also known as "wyrd," from the Norse concept of fate), its appearance in a reading often indicates that there is something the querent is not meant to know yet.

The origin of the blank rune is unclear, but it was popularized by Ralph Blum in the early 1980s. You are of course free to incorporate the blank rune into your divination practice, but because it is clearly not at all a part of the Germanic tradition, it is not part of the interpretations below.

A few technical details are also worth mentioning here. First, the spellings of the rune names in the Elder Futhark, and in some cases the names themselves, can vary wildly. This is because we don't actually have these names in any written evidence from the era of this Futhark—they were reconstructed using the Younger Futhark, the Anglo-Saxon Futhorc, and to some extent the Gothic runes.

Second, the order of two pairs of runes—Eiwhaz and Perthro, and Dagaz and Othala—is reversed in some sources. This is due to inconsistencies in the archeological evidence of the Elder Futhark. Finally, the pronunciations of the names should be taken as approximate, since there are sounds in the Old Norse language that aren't represented by letters in the English alphabet.

FREYR'S AETT

The runes of Freyr's Aett speak to what is needed for basic existence on Earth, for experiencing and interacting with other humans as well as the divine, and for living a fulfilling life.

FEHU

Also known as: Fe, Feh, Feoh, Frey
Pronunciation: fey-who
Letter sound: F
Translation: cattle, wealth, money
Keywords: wealth, prosperity, abundance, reward, good health, beginnings

Primary Themes

The most common interpretation of Fehu concerns wealth—particularly "moveable" wealth. For the ancient Germanic peoples (as well as for many other ancient cultures), to own cattle could mean the difference between a comfortable existence and a life of deprivation. Not only could these animals be traded for other valuable goods, but they offered sustenance in and of themselves and could therefore be life-saving in times of extreme need.

Modern interpretations of Fehu tend to focus on money and credit, as these are the primary sources of "moveable" wealth that we deal with today. However, a broader meaning of this rune concerns prosperity and abundance in general, which includes non-monetary forms of well-being in addition to our reserves of actual cash—good health, plentiful food, love, social success, and a joyful approach to life. Thus, Fehu can serve as a useful reminder to appreciate what is going well in our lives, in whatever form it takes.

Depending on the context of the reading, Fehu may indeed indicate that good fortune in the form of wealth is coming your way. Business success and other kinds of rewards for your efforts are manifesting. However, it also points to the need to share one's good fortune with others in one's family or community. It is important to avoid greed or selfishness in order to maintain positive relationships with others. As the verse for Fehu in the Anglo-Saxon rune poem states, "Wealth is a consolation to all men / Yet much of it must each man give away / If glory he desire / To gain before his god."

Fehu reversed often indicates a loss of wealth, property, or self-esteem. For whatever reason, the winds of fortune are not blowing your way at the moment. You may be experiencing disappointment, frustration, a lack of fulfillment, the need to abandon your plans, or health problems. Regrouping is necessary—what do you need to let go of, and how can you refocus your efforts in a more practical way? This may involve budgeting, cutting back on expenses, taking better care of your body, or reevaluating your priorities. Know that while you may have to deal with some setbacks, this is a learning opportunity, and you will ultimately be better off for having had this experience.

Additional Meanings

As the first character of all the runes in the Elder Futhark, Fehu also symbolizes beginnings. This meaning is reinforced by the rune's literal translation, "cattle," and the Norse myth of Audhumla, the cow who was responsible for creating the father of the human race. Yet as new beginnings always follow endings in the cyclical pattern of life, there is the associated meaning of "completion" here as well.

You may have recently come to the end of a project or endeavor, or otherwise reached a goal you've been working to obtain. If so, you may be being advised to rest and enjoy the fruits of your labor, while still turning your attention to what your next, new focus might be. In this sense, Fehu reversed points to the need to tie up loose ends, commit to finishing an abandoned project, or acknowledge that something has failed and cut your losses.

Because some modern rune systems associate Fehu with Venus and the Moon, it is sometimes associated with romantic love. Depending on the context of the reading, you may be experiencing the beginning relationship, or simply enjoying a period of mutual fulfillment within an established relationship. With Fehu reversed in this context, you may be looking at a break-up, unrequited love, or at the very least a period of dissatisfaction within a relationship.

Magical Uses:

Increase wealth, strengthen psychic ability, attract and improve social relationships, "sending" a magical working into the invisible world to manifest

URUZ

Also known as: Ur, Urz
Pronunciation: oo-rooze
Letter sound: U (as in "brute")
Translation: aurochs (wild European ox), brute strength
Keywords: strength, health, power, energy, endurance, creative force

Primary Themes

In contrast to the domesticated cattle symbolized by Fehu, the second rune of the Elder Futhark represents the aurochs—the wild, fierce European ox of centuries past. This animal was admired for its raw strength, energy, and power, yet because the aurochs was untamable, these qualities were also cause for healthy caution—as were its sharp, deadly horns, which are symbolized by the shape of the rune itself.

This raw strength and power are at the heart of the meaning of Uruz. Physical strength can be indicated, but emotional and spiritual strength are just as likely to be emphasized here. If you are facing challenges, Uruz is a reminder that you have the strength to persevere, as well as to defend yourself from adversaries. If you are pursuing a dream, this rune suggests that there is enough momentum behind you to bring it into manifested form. Summon your connection to divine energy and trust that you will be guided to channel your personal power toward a positive outcome.

A related message is to beware of allowing raw, untamed energy to rule your responses to your situation, or of trying to use your power to control others. Indeed, the challenge presented by Uruz is to "tame" the primal forces of Nature within each of us, so that our energy can be used for everyone's benefit.

Uruz reversed indicates that you have missed opportunities or neglected to recognize your own abilities to achieve success. You may be experiencing a lack of will power or motivation, which can both cause and be caused by a perceived lack of progress. What can you do to restore your self-confidence and proactive energy? What fears—conscious or unconscious—are you allowing to hold you back?

Additional Meanings

Another chief meaning of Uruz relates to health. Upright, this rune indicates that you are or soon will be experiencing good health and a high degree of vitality. Uruz reversed in this respect warns of ill health, low energy, and the need to pay attention to your physical well-being.

Uruz is also a rune of sudden changes, often with unpredictable outcomes. In this context, Uruz upright is encouraging you to weather the upheaval, as new growth and even previously unimagined positive consequences are likely. However, you need to embrace the change and be willing to take chances in order to reap potential rewards. A willingness to engage in "creative risk" is called for here.

Uruz reversed in this interpretation indicates that you are holding back from taking advantage of the opportunities that change and challenges present. If you continue to stand still out of fear of the unknown, you may miss out on something wonderful, and experience stagnation and loss of momentum instead.

Magical Uses:

Bring new circumstances and situations into your experience, strengthen and focus personal will, harness the energy of sudden change to your advantage, healing on all levels, deeper understanding of yourself and underlying motives

THURISAZ

Also known as: Thurs, Thor
Pronunciation: thoo-ree-sahz
Letter sound: TH (as in "thorn")
Translation: thorn, thorn bush, giant, the god Thor
Keywords: protection, warning, contemplation, decisions, luck

Primary Themes

Thurisaz is chiefly concerned with aspects of protection and resistance to danger or other unwanted circumstances. The shape of this rune represents a thorn on a branch, symbolizing the wisdom of choosing a defensive stance, rather than rushing to attack an adversary.

If you go into a challenging or potentially dangerous situation, you can surround yourself with a shield of protective energy, carry a talisman, and/or be extra mindful of your environment and your actions. Taking these measures is often enough to deter potential attackers from trying to harm or take advantage of you, so that you avoid the unpleasant situation altogether. Consider this rune as a friendly but stern warning to be alert to potential danger at this time.

Reversed, Thurisaz in this sense may actually indicate that danger is passing, or that the risk you're facing is less significant. It may also simply point to a feeling of vulnerability or fear of adversity.

In a related interpretation, Thurisaz advises you to be mindful of your motives. Watch out for opportunities that bring reward through deceit or dishonesty, remembering that what goes around comes around. Don't take the "easy path" if doing so allows you to skirt responsibility. Furthermore, be willing to listen to advice from those you trust, even if you don't like what you hear. In this context, drawing Thurisaz reversed may mean that you have been stubborn in this regard, refusing to follow solid advice that could have helped you avoid an unwanted experience.

Additional Meanings

Another common interpretation of Thurisaz indicates that you're facing an important decision requiring careful consideration. Be sure to thoroughly evaluate every aspect of the situation before making your move. Take as much time as you can to decide, and don't make your choice from a place of emotion. The ability to come from a neutral, rational place when making a decision that could significantly impact your life is another form of protection against unwanted circumstances.

Thurisaz reversed may be signaling that you're not serving yourself well in this regard—you may be in denial about an aspect of the situation and therefore unable to make a balanced decision. Seek the advice of experts and/or people whose perspective you trust.

Depending on the context of the reading, Thurisaz can also simply represent a stroke of luck—in either a positive or negative sense, depending on the position of the rune. Thurisaz is sacred to both Thor, the Norse god of thunder and lightning, and Loki, the trickster god. It reminds us that chaos is necessary for transformation, that what appears to be positive at first may not be (and vice versa). We may love a good thunderstorm, and the land may benefit from the rain, but we also know that lightning may strike and trees may be destroyed. Thurisaz represents this destructive, chaotic, primal force within the Universe.

Magical Uses:

Defensive magic, protection, help with decisions, good luck

ANSUZ

Also known as: Ass, As
Pronunciation: ahn-sooze
Letter sound: A (as in "father")
Translation: a god, ancestral god (sometimes interpreted as Odin)
Keywords: communication, wisdom, divine power, a message

Primary Themes

Ansuz is the rune of communication in all its forms, but chiefly verbal communication, whether it involves writing, speaking, or even singing. Messages, advice, or new information may be coming from external sources, or you may be being asked to pay closer attention to the messages coming from your higher self. If you draw Ansuz in a reading related to educational studies or a job interview, this is generally a good omen. This rune also refers to knowledge, reason, and wisdom.

In addition to mundane messages and knowledge, Ansuz is also concerned with divine wisdom and communication with the higher planes. Sacred to Odin, often called the god of wind and spirit, Ansuz hints at the potential for prophecies, revelations, or other messages from your allies in the Otherworld. It may also be pointing to a capacity for spiritual growth and new insights. Be extra open to signals from the Universe in the form of animal sightings, imagery in clouds, numerical messages, and other interesting "coincidences" (better known as "synchronicities").

In the reversed position, Ansuz is associated with the trickster god Loki, and therefore warns you to be on guard against trickery or deceit in communication from others, as well as from your own self. Don't unthinkingly follow advice or believe what you're told simply because you like the message; similarly, don't ignore messages that have importance for your growth simply because you don't want what you're hearing to be true. We are often our own worst "tricksters" in how we perceive and process information from the outside world. Be careful not to misinterpret communications or blindly take things at face value. You may be unable to think reasonably and clearly at this time.

Alternatively, you may be struggling to communicate clearly with others, feeling unsure about your own voice, or feeling cut off from your connection with the divine. You may just need to keep silent and go within for awhile, until you regain clarity, connection, and/or confidence.

Additional Meanings

Chance encounters that lead to new connections, beginnings, and opportunities may be possible now. Keep your eyes and ears open as you socialize with others, whether for business or pleasure. Because of the association between Ansuz and Odin, the father god, this rune can sometimes indicate advice coming from an older, wiser person. Reversed in this context, Ansuz again serves as a warning against being taken in by trickery or deceit by an older person—or by anyone new you encounter.

Many runic systems associate Ansuz with the ash tree, which in Norse tradition is considered the "tree of life," or Yggdrasil ("World Tree"). This tree holds all of the worlds of creation together, representing the divine order of the Universe in all its stability—no matter how chaotic things may look to us from our Earthly perspective at any given time. In this context, Ansuz reminds us that the divine presence is always within and around us, no matter what difficulties we may be facing. If you draw this rune when facing great difficulty, allow it to comfort you, no matter its position.

Magical Uses:

Wisdom, discernment in a complex situation, enhance magical workings, success in dialogue or public speaking, success in examinations, inspiration, divine communication

RAIDHO

Also known as: Reid, Rad
Pronunciation: rye-though
Letter sound: R
Translation: wagon, riding, a vehicle
Keywords: travel, a journey, movement, reunion, changes

Primary Themes

Raidho is the rune of travel, representing both the physical wheel of a wagon, which for so long was the only "vehicle" for traveling in Northern Europe. This rune indicates that you are setting off (or will soon set off) on a journey, whether in the external world or on an emotional or spiritual level.

If your travel is physical, Raidho signals a pleasant experience with few or no mishaps. If you are on a spiritual quest, the going may require significant flexibility on your part, but the rewards of reaching your destination will be well worth it, as you are following your soul's chosen path. Either way, you are advised to keep your focus on the experience of the journey itself, rather than on your arrival. This is because Raidho signifies not just the vehicle you ride in, but also the road you travel on. You will be best served by making the most of every moment along the way.

In reverse, Raidho warns of problems along your journey. This may be in the form of physical breakdowns, delays, or other problems with transit, plans that go awry, or other unpleasant circumstances encountered along the way. If you can postpone your travel, you are advised to do so. If not, be prepared for complications, and remain as flexible and patient as possible. Remember that often times, disruptions and forced changes in our plans can lead to new opportunities we had not imagined. You may be merely being "rerouted" on your journey, to ultimately end up with an even better outcome than hoped for.

Alternatively, you may have to travel for unpleasant reasons, or to a place you would rather not visit. If this is the case, now is a good time to remember that all journeys yield lessons, and you will have an easier time of it if you can be in acceptance as much as possible, rather than in resistance.

Raidho reversed may also signify stagnation on the emotional or spiritual levels—on the journey to self-discovery, your forward motion is presently impeded. You may be avoiding some internal reckoning due to fear of discomfort or emotional pain. However, the discomfort of *not* moving forward as you are meant to will eventually become worse than the process of transformation you are being called to undertake.

Additional Meanings

A related interpretation of Raidho is "reunion"—specifically, the return of old friends in your life or even the arrival of new people with whom you made a soul agreement before incarnating into this life. Alternatively, you may be presented with a chance to resolve a disagreement or conflict, either with someone else or within yourself. Raidho reversed in this context is nudging you to examine how you may be blocking such a reunion or resolution with your attitudes or actions.

Some runic systems also view Raidho as an indicator that now is a good time for negotiations or deliberations related to agreements with others. Raidho reversed advises you to postpone such discussions for now, as other people are not inclined to consider your best interests.

Finally, sometimes Raidho is simply a reminder to align yourself with the "wheel of life" (or in Wiccan terms, the Wheel of the Year). Know that life has ups and downs, ebb and flow, and constant seasonal change. The contrast between opposites is part of the journey of life. If things are not going your way, take heart and know that nothing is permanent.

Magical Uses:

Safe travels, navigating inner journeys, maintaining equanimity in challenging situations, justice in disputes

KENAZ

Also known as: Kano, Ken, Kaun, Kaunan
Pronunciation: kay-nahz
Letter sound: K
Translation: beacon, torch, fire, fire brand
Keywords: light, heat, illumination, breakthrough, creative fire

Primary Themes

In the millennia before electricity was discovered, fire was the only man-made source of heat and light. Kenaz stands for the fire brand, or torch, which people used to heat and illuminate their dwellings, and carried from place to place to light their way. This rune represents the light in the darkness, as well as the warmth that fire provides. On a metaphysical level, this is also the light of knowledge and enlightenment.

Drawing this rune indicates that you are or will be experiencing a breakthrough in some area of your life that has caused you confusion or anguish. Higher guidance is with you now, bringing enlightenment and clarity. You will be able to reconsider your situation in light of new information or understanding, which will allow you to make any necessary changes to your approach. Be sure to take the lessons of your enlightenment to heart. Allow the power and energy of this illuminating experience to open the way for you and propel you along your path.

Reversed, Kenaz indicates that you are feeling left out in the cold or in the dark in some way. You may be experiencing a sense of a spiritual void, or lack of connection to the inner knowledge of your higher self. Often something is ending—a relationship, a career, or some other enterprise. You are advised to trust that this ending is for your highest good. Do not cling to the old circumstances. Know that the period of darkness that comes with endings is necessary, so that a new source of light can come into your life.

Additional Meanings

Kenaz also denotes the fire of creative action and artistry. This is a good time to begin creative projects. Prior obstacles to productivity have been cleared away and you now have optimal energy and passion for your creative work. Harness the power of the forge—where raw materials are transformed into valued objects—to bring your projects to fruition. In this context, Kenaz reversed indicates a lack of creative inspiration and feeling blocked. You may need to tend to your inner self in a different way in order to rekindle the fire.

In a reading centered on romantic situations, Kenaz points to a new relationship beginning, while Kenaz reversed signifies a parting of ways. Often, the emphasis is on the masculine aspects of the relationship. Kenaz reversed can also warn of the destructive powers of fire, such as an unhealthy emphasis on lust or a lack of groundedness in the throes of passion. Keep your balance lest you get burned.

Magical Uses:

Creativity, inspiration, healing, love, balanced relationships, adds power to runic talismans

GEBO

Also known as: Gifu, Gytu
Pronunciation: gay-boo
Letter sound: G (as in "gift")
Translation: gift, hospitality, generosity
Keywords: gift, generosity, friendship, harmony, talents/abilities

Primary Themes

Gebo is the rune of gifts and generosity. Primarily, it signifies an exchange between people that necessarily results in a connection between the giver and receiver. Drawing Gebo often indicates that you are receiving a gift, which may be material in nature or something intangible, such as emotional support.

In centuries past, when contracts were signed by people who couldn't read or write, they made an "x" mark to signify their agreement to the transaction. This concept of agreement between the two parties is a core part of Gebo's meaning. If you are the recipient of a gift from someone else, you choose to either accept or decline it.

Depending on the context of the reading, Gebo may be advising you to accept wholeheartedly with gratitude, or to be wary of the motivations behind the gift. Alternatively, you may be asked to consider your own giving—are you reciprocating sufficiently to honor what you've received? Are you giving away too much, to too many, or to the wrong people?

A related interpretation for Gebo is success and harmony in partnerships. All relationships, whether personal or professional, involve reciprocity to some degree. Drawing this rune indicates that a relationship in your life is blessed with good fortune. With business partners or coworkers, this may mean that a synergy between you leads to productive, enjoyable work. In romance, you may experience a deepening of commitment and passion with your partner.

Just be sure, in all relationships, to pay attention to balance and harmony. Keep both yourself and the other person in mind with all of your actions and decisions. Show compassion to the people in your life, and be able to forgive (another aspect of giving) when forgiveness is needed.

Additional Meanings

Gebo can also refer to gifts from the higher realms, particularly in the context of skills and talents. You may discover a new passion that you have a natural ability for, or further develop a talent you are already pursuing. Drawing this rune is a message of encouragement to keep making the most of what you have been given in order to make your mark on the world.

Gebo has no reversed meaning.

Magical Uses:

Love, sex, harmonious relationships of all kinds, connect with divine energies, boost magical energy and ability

WUNJO

Also known as: Wynja, Wyn
Pronunciation: woon-you
Letter sound: W
Translation: joy, pleasure, hope
Keywords: joy, happiness, harmony, bliss, happy relationships, well-being, success

Primary Themes

A very positive rune, Wunjo literally translates to "joy," and indicates all manner of happiness and well-being. Situations that have been difficult are resolved and optimism is renewed. It may be that a surprise development comes into your life that changes everything for the better. You may experience a feeling of being truly blessed by the higher realms. However, bliss and harmony are also present, and more consistently so, when we take a balanced approach to life.

Constantly focusing on the negative will ultimately bring further negative circumstances—via the Law of Attraction—whereas the practice of recognizing what is going well will not only bring you more well-being, but also means you are feeling satisfied and at peace with your life more of the time. If you have been feeling down, discouraged or irritable, Wunjo may be asking you to adjust your view and focus on what brings you joy. Doing so will allow the positive energy represented by this rune to enter your life.

As the rune of joy, Wunjo is also associated with happy relationships. You are truly enjoying the company of others. Friendships are deepening and romance is successful, whether a relationship is just beginning or is more established.

Wunjo reversed signifies an unhappy time, where things are not going the way you want due to conflict or unexpected problems. You may be lacking energy and interest in life, or stress and anxiety may be dominant in your experience. Avoid making important decisions now, as you are not in a good frame of mind to choose the best course, or to even be aware of all of your options.

In relationships, there may be tension or misunderstandings, possibly leading to arguments or even the end of the partnership. If you can, take some time out to let the negative energies subside and return to the issue with a clearer, calmer mind and heart.

Additional Meanings

Wunjo is considered a good sign when it comes to business and prosperity, as well as the rewards of following your ambition in general. You are enjoying your work, especially if you are involved in something creative. Now may be a good time to start a new venture, depending on the other runes in the reading.

Wunjo reversed in this context warns that now is not a good time for new projects, or may simply indicate that your ambition has been blocked by real or perceived obstacles or interference. You may be dissatisfied with your job or with the results of your work. If this is the case, focus as much as you can on other areas of your life that bring you joy. In this way, you can balance your outlook on life and make more room for new, positive developments to come in.

Magical Uses:

General well-being, fulfillment, success, raise vibrational frequency, harmonious relationships of all kinds, powerful in bind runes

HAGAL'S AETT

The runes of Hagal's Aett speak to the unavoidable experiences of life—disruption, change, stalled progress, and even unexpected luck. They help us navigate the more difficult aspects of our life's path and remind us that nothing lasts forever.

HAGALAZ

Also known as: Hagal, Hagall
Pronunciation: hah-gah-lahz
Letter sound: H
Translation: hail, hailstone
Keywords: destruction, chaos, interference, misfortune, transformation

Primary Themes

The first rune of Hagal's Aett translates to "hail," and points to the fact that we cannot always control our circumstances. Even with all of the technology we possess in modern times, Nature can step in at any moment with destructive forces that flatten cities and even countries. Hailstorms may be brief and localized compared to larger natural disasters, but the balls of ice that pelt the ground can leave destruction in their wake, injuring people and animals and destroying entire crops.

This certainly would have spelled disaster for any ancient community living off of the land.

Hagalaz signifies these forces of chaos that cannot be controlled, whether they come in the form of sweeping disaster, illness, or simply unexpected problems or disruptions that interfere with your progress toward a goal. You cannot control or "fix" this interference—in other words, resistance is futile. While this may be a frustrating time, know that your course is being corrected for reasons beyond your understanding. You may be being forced into taking a new approach, which will become clear with patience and perseverance, as well as an ability to analyze your situation without attachment to the outcome.

If the reading is generally positive, then the chaos may be interpreted at the lower end of the spectrum—a temporary interruption rather than an unexpected, life-altering development. If the runes close to Hagalaz are negative, then the trouble may be more severe or have long-lasting implications. If your reading is about a new project or endeavor, you may not want to start just yet.

Additional Meanings

Hail is a temporary phenomenon, beginning and ending as water in a liquid state. Hagalaz can signify a significant change that may be rocky at first, but ultimately the transformation that results from this experience will leave you better off. Important shifts are taking place for you, whether materially, emotionally, or spiritually. But for new creation to occur, what is old must be dismantled.

Hagalaz has no reversed meaning.

Magical Uses:

Protection, luck, quick transformations, success in navigating difficult situations, break unhealthy patterns

NAUTHIZ

Also known as: Naud, Naudirz, Not, Nautiz, Nied
Pronunciation: now-theez
Letter sound: N
Translation: need, necessity
Keywords: need, necessity, scarcity, absence, restriction, have patience

Primary Themes

Nauthiz signifies hardship in the form of one's needs not being met, whether this indicates poverty, hunger, unemployment, lack of good health, or lack of emotional support. The rune stave represents the "need-fire," a ritual fire lit from two large beams of wood that ancient Northern Europeans would light in times of extreme hardship or disaster, such as a famine or outbreak of fatal disease.

You may be experiencing hardship that limits your ability to move forward or live comfortably, or a strong desire that appears impossible to fulfill. The possibilities are restricted due to your lack of resources, and you are likely chafing at the constraints and/or disheartened by your circumstances. The Anglo-Saxon rune poem describes Nauthiz as "a tight band across the chest," which is often how need and restriction feel.

The advice of this rune is to treat this situation as a period of learning and an opportunity to strengthen your resilience. No one enjoys hardship while it's happening, but when we look back on the experiences that made us who we are, generally at least a few of them were unpleasant. Don't allow bitterness, worry, or despair to get the best of you, but rather use your gifts and talents to find ways to get your needs met. Remember that needs and limitations are necessary for growth, as we would never learn or accomplish anything significant if we always had everything we needed or wanted at all times.

There are conflicting viewpoints among rune readers as to whether Nauthiz has a reverse position. Many traditions hold that it does not, but the rune stave is not at all symmetrical and the difference between its upright and upside down positions can be fairly clearly distinguished.

Either way, those who recognize "Nauthiz reversed" do not interpret it as the opposite of its "upright" meaning, but rather assign some aspects of its overall meaning to the reversed position. These are found below in "additional meanings." If your intuition suggests that a reverse meaning for Nauthiz reversed should be distinctly recognized, these interpretations can serve for this rune in this position. If not, then the context provided by the other runes and the question guiding the reading can shed light on what Nauthiz is telling you at this time.

Additional Meanings

Nauthiz may be warning you to avoid greed or unhealthy desire, which can lead to destructive behaviors and negative consequences. If you have been focusing too heavily on the material world, this is a sign to go within and tend to your spiritual development.

This rune may also be a warning against making hasty decisions or committing to something at this time, as unexpected needs or limitations may result. You are advised to conserve your energy, focusing only on the essentials for now. You are likely simply not at the right place or time for moving forward. Patience is the best strategy.

Nauthiz has no reversed meaning.

Magical Uses:

Protection, maintaining equanimity in difficult circumstances, activates magical workings focused on attraction or increase

92

ISA

Also known as: Isaz, Isa, Is, Iss, Isarz
Pronunciation: ee-sah
Letter sound: I (as in "ice")
Translation: ice
Keywords: obstacles, standstill, stagnation, delay, coldness

Primary Themes

Isa is the third rune in Hagal's Aett, and the third in a row to carry a predominantly negative meaning. It translates literally to "ice," which may seem, depending on the context, to be a neutral or even positive substance to modern people, but to the ancient people of Northern Europe, ice was useless, and was more often than not an obstacle.

As a representation of frozen water, Isa signifies a lack of movement which is likely frustrating. There may be physical circumstances blocking your progress, a loss of energy, or mental blocks that you cannot see past in order to move forward.

Isa also indicates delay, and it is best to accept this as a reality in your current situation, rather than pushing against it. Know that the sun will eventually return to melt the ice and allow the water to flow freely again. In the meantime, take advantage of this still, static energy to practice focusing on the present moment. Meditation is highly useful now, as it can help dissipate frustration and take your focus off of things you can't control.

Don't give up on your ambition or assume that a delay means it won't work out. If there's anything you can do to prepare for making progress once it becomes possible again, put your energy there instead. You might even find that you're better equipped to pursue your goal as a result.

Additional Meanings

In the context of relationships, Isa can also point to emotional coldness between people. This could pertain to friendships, family relationships, or romantic partnerships. Affection may be lacking, communication may have come to a standstill, or a passionate romance may be cooling off. Arguments or conflicts are either present or forthcoming.

Ask yourself if you have been open and demonstrative of your feelings for the person or people in question. If it is they who have closed themselves off, consider how you might approach reconnecting or rekindling the energy between you. Recognize, however, that in some situations, it may be best to let go and move on.

The transparency of ice can also signify clarity, whether it comes to relationships or any other situation causing difficulty. Evaluating your circumstances from a cool, emotionally detached viewpoint can be helpful now, which is one positive aspect of Isa.

Isa has no reversed meaning.

Magical Uses:

Maintaining the status quo, protection against unwanted energies or developments, bringing clarity to a situation

---

JERA

Also known as: Jara, Jeran, Jeraz
Pronunciation: yair-ah
Letter sound: Y (as in "year") (J in Germanic languages)
Translation: year, harvest
Keywords: harvest, reward, natural cycles, fruition, fertility, growth

Primary Themes

Jera is the rune of harvest, and of the seasonal year which is ever turning. Similar to the Neopagan concept of the Wheel of the Year, Jera signifies that each season of a cycle has its purpose, and so it also reminds us that the attainment of goals often takes time. A seed planted in spring must be given time to grow, and the resulting plant can only be harvested in its proper time. But provided you have put the necessary work into preparing the soil, tending the crops, and reaping the harvest, Jera indicates that your efforts will be successful.

As the fourth rune in Hagal's Aett, Jera follows the series of three runes which focused on obstacles. If you have been dealing with adversity, Jera emerges as a positive sign that troubles are receding and you are moving into a fortuitous time of forward activity. This is a rune of reaping rewards for hard work and perseverance. It may indicate prosperity and abundance, success in business, or some other form of payoff for your efforts. Celebrate your good fortune, appreciate the joys of your current circumstances, and strengthen your hopes and plans for the future.

Don't rest on your laurels for too long, however. Just as the work of preparing for winter must follow close on the heels of the harvest celebrations, the need for careful resourcefulness and quiet patience will come around again in due time. This is simply the natural, cyclical order of life. Recognizing this helps you to flow with circumstances rather than resisting them.

Additional Meanings

As a rune of growth cycles, Jera also represents fertility and may indicate a marriage. Procreation may be indicated—either in the form of literal pregnancy or in the growth of an enterprise. Some Neopagan traditions associate this rune with the symbolic sacred union of the Goddess and the God.

At any rate, Jera symbolizes the union of "opposites," such as dawn and dusk (the meeting points of night and day) and the liminal times between seasons, such as the warm days of autumn days or the cold days of spring. In this context, you are advised to acknowledge that any adversity you are or have been experiencing will ultimately contribute to your growth—you are who you are because of the lessons life has taught you.

Jera has no reversed meaning.

Magical Uses:

Fertility, creativity, bringing in desired events, family matters, growth and increase, patience, facilitates harmonious relationship to time and seasons

---
EIHWAZ

Also known as: Eoh, Eow, Ihwaz, Iwarz
Pronunciation: eeh-wahz
Letter sound: uncertain (possibly "E" as in "need" or "A" as in "cat")
Translation: yew
Keywords: death, regeneration, rebirth, changes, magic

Primary Themes

Eihwaz represents the yew tree, making it symbolic of both death and regeneration. The yew is a highly toxic plant to humans and livestock, and poisons made from the tree were used for both murder and suicide in ancient times. However, yew is also considered a tree of life, due to its evergreen nature and its extreme longevity—a wild yew tree can live for thousands of years. When they do begin to die, they can be regenerated by their own "daughter trees" that grow inside their decaying trunks. This combination of qualities makes the yew— and its representative rune, Eihwaz—an extremely powerful symbol of the cycle of death and life.

Eihwaz doesn't indicate literal death, but rather an ending that will lead to a new beginning. If things seem to be at a halt, be patient. You are being asked to allow an old situation to fall away, so that new developments can come into your life. Alternatively, you may be experiencing a metaphorical "death" in the form of leaving behind old ways, allowing old aspects of yourself to die away now that they are no longer serving you. Don't resist the changes that are underway— rather, learn to "go with the flow" and be flexible. You may not be able to see it now, but what you are currently dealing with is paving the way for a new and improved situation.

Eihwaz is often compared to the Death card in the Tarot, though the runes as we know them precede the Tarot by at least a thousand years. Interestingly, both carry the number 13—the Death card is the 13th in the Major Arcana and Eihwaz is the 13th rune in the Elder Futhark. Like Eihwaz, the Death card is as much about regeneration and new beginnings as it is about endings. Eihwaz is also positioned in the middle of the runic alphabet, signifying that "death" is only the end of a cycle, and never the end of the story.

Additional Meanings

As a symbol of the yew and of regeneration, Eihwaz is also associated with magical work, particularly of a protective nature and/or in dealing with transformation. It has been called a symbol of the gateway to the underworld, and of deliberate "journeys" to the non-physical realm in search of knowledge or understanding. According to some scholars, the rune is more of a magical symbol than a "letter," as it is rarely seen in actual runic writing.

In this context, Eihwaz may indicate that you have more power than you realize to navigate the changes you're experiencing, and you may be able to actively facilitate your transformation rather than simply waiting for external forces to change.

In some readings, Eihwaz may point to an aspect of your past that you have not resolved. Until you do, this incident, relationship, or other circumstance will continue to hinder you. Address it now so that you can fully move forward.

Eihwaz has no reversed meaning.

Magical Uses:

Protection, overcoming obstacles, spiritual development, strengthen personal and magical power, good banishing rune, divination, past-life recall

---

PERTHRO

Also known as: Perdhro, Pertho, Pertra, Perthu
Pronunciation: pair-throh
Letter sound: P
Translation: [unknown]
Keywords: mystery, secrets, revelation, chance

Primary Themes

Of all the runes, Perthro is the most mysterious. Its meaning has never been agreed upon by scholars, but the symbol is often interpreted as a receptacle used for casting lots, such as a modern-day dice cup. As such, Perthro is associated with divination and the use of the runes as a means of discovering hidden knowledge.

Drawing Perthro can indicate that things are not quite as they seem, and that something previously unknown is about to be revealed. This could be a secret someone has been keeping, or it could be a spiritual truth that has been hidden from you until now. You are advised to pay attention to the signs and signals that your intuition is picking up on. Now is also a good time to pursue any esoteric interests, such as learning more about magic or about communication with the higher realms.

If you've been wrestling with a stubborn conundrum, Perthro may be signaling a need to go within to find the answers you're seeking. Spend time meditating, go for a long walk, or find other ways to attune with the Universal energies that get obscured by the mental clutter of modern life. Clearing your mind allows the enlightenment you need to arise naturally, without effort. Trust in the mysteries of the unknown, and all will be revealed in due time.

Perthro reversed may indicate an unpleasant surprise or revelation. It could also point to a secret that you are holding onto, which is becoming harder to keep, or an unhealthy focus on something from the past. Alternatively, it may be cautioning you not to expect too much at this time, or to get attached to outcomes. You may be wasting energy by focusing on external circumstances rather than allowing your happiness to come from within. If the overall reading is unclear, Perthro reversed may be telling you to hold off from divination for now, and come back to the runes at a later time.

Alternate Meanings

Perthro can also be interpreted as "chance," in the sense of a surprise or an unexpected positive development. In this context, Perthro reversed indicates potential disappointment, so avoid taking risks at this time, especially involving money.

Depending on the context of the reading, Perthro can also point to fertility, pregnancy, and/or birth, as the receptive shape of the symbol has been associated with the womb. Some Neopagan traditions view Perthro as the womb of the Mother Goddess, bringing forth life from the non-physical realms into physical form here on Earth. Perthro reversed in this sense can point to sexual or reproductive difficulties.

Magical Uses:

Good luck in gambling, protect business investments, divination, health and healing, foster spiritual clarity, fertility

---

ELHAZ

Also known as: Algiz, Eoih, Elgr
Pronunciation: el-hahz
Letter sound: Z
Translation: protection, elk, sedge plant
Keywords: protection, defense, opportunity

Primary Themes

Elhaz is the rune of defense and protection. Its shape is said to represent both the elk, with its imposing antlers, and the sedge plant, whose sharp leaves act as natural protection from would-be predators. Both images illustrate the power represented by this rune—a built-in protective force that discourages negative influences from affecting your personal experience.

Drawing Elhaz indicates that you are safe from danger and that there is no need to fear. However, don't take the protective energy for granted by being reckless with your actions, as this rune does not mean that there is no danger present whatsoever. It simply means that as long as you remain alert and clear-minded and in touch with your intuition, you are headed for a positive outcome. Elhaz has also been interpreted as a symbol of reaching up to connect with the divine for support. By listening to your higher guidance, you will know which moves to make to stay out of harm's way.

Elhaz reversed may indicate that you have been doing just the opposite—losing touch with your intuition or even your common sense. You are advised to be on guard for any trouble that may be coming toward you while you've been disconnected from your higher guidance. There is a sense of vulnerability around you at this time, with the potential for danger or negative influences coming from an unexpected direction.

Don't become paranoid or paralyzed with fear, however, as these reactions block your clarity and can prevent you from navigating the situation safely. Make sure you are taking care of your physical, mental, and emotional health at this time, and avoid making rushed decisions.

Additional Meanings

Elhaz can also refer to an upcoming opportunity or quest. Usually this involves one or more other people, who may bring an offer or an invitation to join in a venture of some kind. As long as your intuition agrees, go for it—this is a favorable time for a new endeavor and it is likely to produce positive results at a rapid pace. If the central question of the reading relates to new ventures—particularly one involving risk, then Elhaz is an indicator of good fortune.

On the other hand, Elhaz reversed in this context warns that someone may be trying to take advantage of you. Be wary of both business and romantic relationships with people you have just met or don't know very well. Investigate all the possible angles and don't hesitate to decline an offer if anything seems "off." Remember, your intuition is your protection when Elhaz comes into play.

Magical Uses:

Protection from negative energy and people, protection of property, strengthen friendships, astral communication

SOWILO

Also known as: Sowulu, Sol, Sunna
Pronunciation: so-we-loh
Letter sound: S
Translation: Sun
Keywords: light, energy, good health, success

Primary Themes

Sowilo is the rune of the Sun and the life-sustaining light it provides. While Kenaz represents the light of the torch fire, guiding one through the night, Sowilo represents the light of day, in which all is illuminated and there is no darkness to obscure our vision. It is the rune of the light's victory over the dark and can bring much needed clarity and healing to a situation.

Sowilo's verse in the Anglo-Saxon rune poem describes the sun as "a joy in the hopes of seafarers," keeping sailors' spirits up as they move across the water toward safe landing. Sowilo is telling you that you are surrounded by warmth and light. Success, good health, and joy are yours if you will allow yourself to have them, as are good luck and prosperity. Depending on your situation, however, you may need to open yourself up more and clear out your own inner shadows to let more light (and life) into your experience.

Drawing Sowilo indicates that you are in a position to use the beneficial energies of the Sun to illuminate your path and reach your goals. Draw on your creativity and your inherent skills and talents to strengthen your pursuits, knowing that you have great power at your disposal.

Additional Meanings

While the Sun is crucial to life on Earth, its power can also be harmful if its intensity is not balanced with other forms of energy. Depending on the context of the reading, Sowilo may be asking you to look at how you are directing your vitality. Are you scattered over too many activities or commitments? Are you neglecting your health or at risk of burning out? Be sure to cool off and ground yourself when necessary, so you can continue utilizing the Sun's power for positive results.

Alternatively, you may be making something out to be bigger or more significant than it really is, or placing yourself in the spotlight when it would be more prudent to step back from a situation. Use the Sun's power to illuminate the issue with rational clarity rather than through the lens of emotions. Be honest with yourself and with others, as deceit keeps everyone in the shadows.

Sowilo has no reversed meaning.

Magical Uses:

Strengthen self-confidence, motivation, success, healing, victory over challenges, spiritual guidance

TYR'S AETT

The runes of Tyr's Aett speak to aspects of the dance between the visible and invisible realms, with runes directly connected to ancient deities, natural forces, and humanity itself.

TIWAZ

Also known as: Teiwaz, Tyr, Tiwar
Pronunciation: tee-wahz
Letter sound: T
Translation: the god Tyr
Keywords: courage, victory, strength, passion, masculine energy

Primary Themes

As the first rune in Tyr's Aett, Tiwaz represents the qualities of the god Tyr, and is associated with courage, strength, and the forward-moving nature of masculine energy. Tyr proved his bravery and dedication to his community of gods by sacrificing his right hand in order to keep the Fenris Wolf from harming Odin.

As such, Tiwaz speaks of the need to put our causes above our personal desires if the greater good requires it. If you are facing a decision that involves potential discomfort in order to achieve a positive outcome, Tiwaz is signalling that you possess the courage and the ability to withstand the sacrifice and emerge victorious. You are ready for the challenge, provided you act with integrity and remain true to your inner knowledge. Stand your ground and keep the faith, and your ultimate success will be recognized and respected by others.

Victory is another primary interpretation of Tiwaz, particularly when it comes to competitions of all kinds. You are likely feeling enthusiastic and motivated at this time—harness this energy toward achieving your goals and you will succeed. This rune is also a positive sign for success in legal matters, provided that you are being honest and just in your actions.

The shape of Tiwaz resembles a spear—a symbol associated with Tyr—as well as an upward-pointing arrow, both of which symbolize the force of masculine energy. Action is indicated, rather than passivity, though you are cautioned not to act impulsively or let your determination override your intuition.

Tiwaz can also indicate a male person. If the querent is male, then Tiwaz generally represents him. If the querent is female, Tiwaz often represents a male close to her—a partner, family member, or close friend. In this context, the runes closest to Tiwaz in the reading have direct influence on the person being represented.

Tiwaz reversed points to a lack of courage or motivation when it comes to achieving your goals. You may be disheartened or even depressed by the appearance of obstacles in your way. You are most likely experiencing a blockage of forward-moving energy, making it impossible to gain traction in any direction. Alternatively, you may be moving too quickly—making hasty decisions that will cost you in the long run. You might even be displaying obstinate inflexibility, refusing to consider any ideas other than your own.

No matter the circumstances, the advice of Tiwaz reversed is the same: slow down. Take your time, consider all of your options, listen to any advice offered by others, and make sure you're grounded and centered before proceeding again.

Additional Meanings

Another aspect of the masculine energy of Tiwaz is passion and sexual energy, so romance is also indicated by this rune, depending on the context of the reading. This may refer to a new romance, or a reinvigoration of an existing relationship.

Reversed in this context, Tiwaz can point to a fizzling of passion or even dishonest behavior on the part of a romantic partner—especially a male partner. Communication may be strained or nonexistent. You may need to decide whether the relationship is worth whatever it's costing you to remain in it.

Magical Uses:

Healing, success, victory in competitions, strengthen willpower, courage, healthy masculine energy, strengthen spiritual faith

---

BERKANA

Also known as: Berkano, Bairkan, Beorc, Bjarkan
Pronunciation: bair-kah-nah
Letter sound: B
Translation: birch, birch goddess
Keywords: birth, new beginnings, family, growth, regeneration

Primary Themes

A very positive rune, Berkana symbolizes new beginnings. This can take the form of a new project, a new relationship, a new phase of spiritual development, or a new idea that leads to successful outcomes. The Universal energies are fertile and lined up for bringing forth new manifestations, so you are in an excellent position to begin your next adventure. Berkana is known as the birth rune, and can indicate the actual birth of a child, a wedding, or other happy family occasion. This rune is a very good sign for women who are trying to conceive.

Berkana is the rune of female energy and its shape represents the breasts of the archetypal Earth Mother, who was known in many different guises to pagan cultures around the globe. This rune symbolizes the nurturing, attentive, and protective qualities of maternal energy.

Depending on the context of the reading, Berkana may be asking you to look at where your own caretaking energy is being directed. Are you nurturing your dreams and goals? Are you taking good care of yourself? Alternatively, it could be pointing to a supportive outside influence—whether a person or an environment—that can be helpful to you now. Don't be afraid to accept loving assistance from others.

Berkana can also signify a female person. If the querent is female, then Berkana generally represents her. If the querent is male, Tiwaz often represents a female close to him—a partner, family member, or close friend. In this context, the runes closest to Berkana in the reading have direct influence on the person being represented.

In the reverse position, Berkana points to stagnation and obstacles to beginning something new. Depending on the context, it may indicate trouble conceiving or issues with pregnancy, or with getting a new enterprise off the ground. There may be conflicts within the home or family, with tempers flaring easily. You may be worrying about someone you love, or offering support to someone who won't accept it.

The advice here is to keep an open mind, and perhaps reexamine the motives behind your actions. But don't block yourself off to new possibilities by focusing on things you can't change. Focus your energy where you can be productive, and give the intractable problems a rest.

Additional Meanings

Berkana's translation is "birch," a highly revered tree associated with renewal and regeneration. The birch was among the first trees that returned to reforest the land after the last Ice Age, and is one of the first trees to leaf out in the spring.

If you're struggling with difficulties or if the reading is predominantly negative, drawing Berkana is a reminder that no matter how cold or dark things may seem, warmth and light will return. You may very well be in a dormant phase that precedes a spiritual reawakening. Soon enough, you will begin to bloom again.

Magical Uses:

Fertility, female health, strengthen family ties, love, protection, bringing ideas into physical manifestation, creativity

EHWAZ

Also known as: Ehwass, Eih, Eoh
Pronunciation: ay-wahz
Letter sound: E ("eh," as in "element")
Translation: horse
Keywords: changes, faith, loyalty, trust, movement, travel

Primary Themes

The shape of Ehwaz is symbolic of the horse, revered as a sacred animal in the cultures of the ancient Germanic tribes. This rune represents the qualities of faith, loyalty, and trust—all necessary to a successful relationship between a horse and its rider.

Ehwaz is a rune of partnership and friendship, and indicates the need to be faithful and accountable to the people in your life. If the reading is about a relationship, drawing Ehwaz is a good sign that these crucial aspects are present for both people involved.

The concept of faithfulness also applies to yourself and your goals. If your reading is about a specific pursuit, Ehwaz is reminding you that you have what it takes to accomplish it, but you must dedicate yourself fully to the endeavor in order to see it through. Steady progress is made by placing one foot in front of the other. Provided you do your part, the support you need will arise and you will gain momentum.

Depending on the context of the reading, Ehwaz in the reversed position could indicate that you or someone else in a relationship is not demonstrating faith or loyalty. If you have been wondering whether to trust someone, Ehwaz reversed may be confirming your doubts. Alternatively, it may be signalling a lack of faith or trust on your part. This is a good time to step back and take a look at the bigger picture—are you harboring past hurts that are preventing you from trusting or accepting someone else's trust?

If the reading is related to a goal, Ehwaz reversed indicates a lack of momentum. Take an objective look at how you have been approaching things up to now. Is there a lack of faith in yourself or in the outcome that's keeping you stuck? If so, don't make decisions from this place—wait until you've regained your confidence.

Additional Meanings

Horses are able to change direction swiftly, and another meaning for Ehwaz is change. Often this is in the form of changing jobs or place of residence. This is a positive change, even if it may seem daunting at first.

Ehwaz reversed in this context may be signalling that you are ready for change in a specific situation, due to feeling constrained or restless.

Depending on the other runes in the reading, it may be an indication that it's time to start exploring your options.

Ehwaz is also associated with movement and travel, as horses were key means of transportation in the ancient world. This can be a journey in the physical world, but is likely an internal, spiritual journey, as horses are associated with astral travel in many shamanic traditions around the world. If you have been experiencing severe emotional or physical difficulties, Ehwaz may be indicating that you are actually on an inner journey toward a transformed and stronger self than you were before. Keep an open mind in order to learn the spiritual lessons that your life is presenting to you now.

Ehwaz reversed in the context of physical travel is a warning that now is not the best time to go on a journey. If you can avoid traveling, do so. If not, just take extra care and don't let interruptions or "bumps in the road" get to you. In the context of a spiritual journey, Ehwaz reversed warns against trying to wriggle out of the inner work through escapism, whether in the form of substance abuse, workaholism, or mind-numbing technology.

Magical Uses:

Safe travels, physical and mental stamina, promotes trustworthy and loyal relationships, brings swift change, aids with astral travel

MANNAZ

Also known as: Madr, Madir, Mann
Pronunciation: mah-nahz
Letter sound: M

Translation: man, mankind, human
Keywords: humanity, the self, support, assistance, intelligence, family

Primary Themes

Mannaz is the rune of humankind, and symbolizes the characteristics that set humans apart from the rest of the Earth's living creatures: the ability to create for the sake of creativity itself, to develop and contribute to culture, to read and write, etc. This rune reminds us that we are part of a shared experience among all humans, no matter our specific language, physical appearance, or beliefs. At the same time, Mannaz represents the self, with particular emphasis on one's inner being.

Often, this rune is pointing to some aspect of tension in the relationship between your inner self and your perceived place in the outer world. You may be feeling at odds with the attitudes and expectations of society. If this is the case, be sure you are listening to your intuition—rather than your ego—to determine the best course of action. Mannaz reminds you to maintain self-awareness, checking in with yourself physically, emotionally and spiritually as you choose how to respond to your circumstances.

In addition to emphasizing the inner self, Mannaz also symbolizes assistance from others. Its shape evokes a sense of mutual support, as in two individuals coming together to stabilize each other, creating a stronger structure as a result. You may be on the receiving end of assistance from someone else, or asked to lend support to a common cause. Be sure to remain open to help from others at this time, and willing to lend a hand where needed. Independence and self-reliance are important attributes, but ultimately, humans need each other in order to reach their full potential.

In the reversed position, Mannaz can be pointing to isolation, low self-esteem, and/or self-preoccupation. You may be out of alignment with your inner self, and needing some "down time" away from others in order to tune back in. Or you might be feeling like an "outcast" over a particular social conflict. Take some time to honestly examine the role you've played in the issue, and prepare to make any necessary amends once the situation cools a bit.

Mannaz reversed may also indicate that you are not likely to receive assistance from anyone else just now, or are even experiencing interference from others regarding a goal you're working toward. If so, self-reliance and unconventional approaches are useful at this time.

Depending on its position in the reading, Mannaz may represent the querent. If this is the case, the runes closest to Mannaz have the strongest direct influence on the querent.

Additional Meanings

In connection with the theme of "humanity," Mannaz also symbolizes human intelligence and creativity. It is considered a *hugrune*, or a rune of the mind, and indicates success in matters related to language, law, and academic studies. Reversed in this context, Mannaz is warning you that you are missing some crucial element of common sense in your approach to the issue at hand.

Mannaz can also refer to family matters, and may indicate that you are concerned about someone close to you—either blood family or chosen family. In this context, Mannaz reversed advises you to take some time away from the problem and focus on keeping yourself balanced and healthy. After all, you can't set yourself on fire to keep someone else warm. Recharge your emotional batteries so that you will be available to assist when and if the time is right.

Magical Uses:

Help or cooperation from others, increase mental agility, improve memory, promote harmonious relationships, success in legal and academic issues

LAGUZ

Also known as: Lagu, Laguz, Lagaz, Logr
Pronunciation: lah-gooze
Letter sound: L
Translation: water
Keywords: water, flow, intuition, the unconscious, psychic ability, the feminine, growth

Primary Themes

Laguz is the water rune, symbolizing the element in all of its forms: rivers, streams, lakes, seas, and oceans, the rain, and even the water contained within our bodies. It is also connected to emotions, the cleansing of unwanted energy through tears, and the unpredictability of life.

If you are being tossed around in the emotional waters of a situation, Laguz advises you to release your resistance and go with the flow. Adaptability is key here, as continuing to resist your circumstances will only plunge you further into disharmony. The same is true when it comes to positive circumstances—acknowledge and enjoy them with gratitude, but don't cling to them as the source of your happiness. Let the fluidity of life guide you, rather than trying to control and direct it.

As the rune of water, Laguz is also the rune of intuition and the subconscious. You may be getting a lot of intuitive hits from your inner self right now. Be sure to follow your "gut," even if your brain is telling you differently. Laguz indicates psychic ability which can be nurtured and strengthened with practice. Stay open and receptive to the messages coming in from the spirit world and your higher self. Trust your own inner process to help you navigate any stormy seas.

Laguz reversed points to a lack of flow in your life, perhaps from feeling stagnated in a current job or relationship, or simply from neglecting your intuitive and spiritual side. You may be blocking some unpleasant emotions that need to be allowed to come through in order for you to move forward. Alternatively, you may be feeling tempted to give in to unhealthy impulses or take the "easy route" regarding a situation, which will not lead to the spiritual growth you are meant to experience. Whatever the case, spending some time in or near a natural body of water can help you find clarity and courage, and is highly beneficial to your energy at this time.

Additional Meanings

Laguz is also symbolic of feminine energy and can represent the woman in the context of male-female relationships. Feminine strength and support are indicated here.

Reversed in this context, Laguz can point to a woman in your life who has hidden ulterior motives or is in some way a source of trouble for you at this time. Stay in touch with your own intuition in dealings with this person.

Creativity and growth are further aspects of this rune. Laguz is sometimes translated to mean "leek," an edible and magical herb revered by the ancient Norse. Leeks grew wild in Northern Europe and were considered symbols of growth and virility. In this context, Laguz represents the life force found within all matter on Earth. If you have been hiding or ignoring a creative talent, this rune is nudging you to develop it, as it will facilitate further growth in your life.

Conversely, Laguz reversed may indicate that you are experiencing a lack of creativity. You may need to shake things up a bit and get out of your normal routine in order to allow new creative energy into your life.

Magical Uses:

Increase intuitive and psychic abilities, healthy feminine energy, creativity, maintaining equanimity in difficult situations

---

INGWAZ

Also known as: Inguz, Enguz, Ing
Pronunciation: eeng-wahz
Letter sound: NG (as in "wing")
Translation: the god Ing (also known as Ingwaz)
Keywords: fertility, male procreative force, channeling energy, completion, safety

Primary Themes

Ingwaz is the rune of the fertility god Ing (also known as Ingwaz), and is associated with masculine sexuality and male potency. This is the springtime energy of plant life emerging after the depths of winter, and the procreation of all life on Earth. Depending on context of the reading, drawing Ingwaz may indicate a healthy and hearty sexual relationship.

However, it can also refer more generally to a procreative energy being channeled through specific means, such as a project, a business endeavor, or a journey. Whatever is propelling you forward in a positive way at the moment, Ingwaz is acknowledging and confirming that the energy behind it is potent and heading for substantial results.

As a related meaning, Ingwaz also symbolizes completion. An old phase of your life is coming to an end, freeing up the energy for new phenomena to enter your experience. Problems are resolved or about to be solved, and great relief follows.

Alternatively, Ingwaz may be signalling that you are reaching your full potential in the matter at hand and that it's time to let go and let the situation play itself out. Trust that you have done the necessary work—the energy you're feeling around this is ultimately positive, and relief is in sight.

Ingwaz is widely considered a highly auspicious rune, signalling a major event or turning point in your life that leads to satisfying results. A dream may very well be coming true.

Additional Meanings

Ing is also a god of the home and hearth, and so Ingwaz indicates safety and a loving family environment. Your home and everyone in it are protected. If you were feeling anxiety about some kind of threat to your well-being in this regard, you can relax. Enjoy a sense of peace, prosperity, and satisfaction with your life at this time. This is indeed a rune of good fortune.

Ingwaz has no reversed meaning.

Magical Uses:

Fertility, bringing a situation to an end, building and releasing magical energy, protection, passion

DAGAZ

Also known as: Daeg, Dags, Dogr
Pronunciation: dah-gahz
Letter sound: D
Translation: day
Keywords: daylight, success, hope, breakthrough, transformation, balance

Primary Themes

Dagaz is the rune of daylight and is considered a very beneficial sign in any reading. For the ancient Norse, daylight was a precious commodity during the long, cold winters. Dagaz is associated with the contrasting blessing of midsummer, when the days are long and the Sun is at its height of power.

Increase, growth, prosperity, strength, good health, and general well-being are indicated by this rune. You may experience an unexpected successful outcome concerning a problem or project you have been working on. You are encouraged to remain optimistic and to keep your focus on the light as positive new developments unfold.

Dagaz is also known as the "dawn rune," and as such represents new hope, and an emerging from darkness into light. You may have recently undergone a "dark night" on a physical, emotional, or spiritual level, and are now able to greet the new day with a hard-won clarity and confidence.

There is a related aspect of protection to Dagaz, as daylight is considered a protective force, guiding us out of danger and onto the right path and keeping unwanted influences at bay. You are out of harm's way now, so you can rejoice in safety and look forward to new openings and opportunities.

As the first light of dawn breaks through the dark of night, Dagaz also represents the breakthrough of insight and inspiration, whether on an artistic, creative level or in terms of spiritual enlightenment. This rune may be pointing to a time when you have access to communion with divine energies, perhaps even psychic knowledge of situations or events that eludes everyone else involved.

Whatever the case, spiritual development and advancement are indicated here. Divine light is guiding you along your path and you are making steady progress.

Additional Meanings

The symmetrical shape of Dagaz represents balance between opposing energies—light and dark, up and down, movement and stagnation, etc. Depending on the context of the reading, this rune may be reminding you to seek more balance in your approach to a problem or in your daily life in general.

Alternatively, Dagaz can point to a major transformation or fundamental change in your life. Some have compared the rune's shape to the wings of a butterfly, evoking the beautiful, winged completion of what can start out as an uncomfortable or frightening transition. If you are feeling immobilized or uprooted by major changes in your life, let Dagaz be a reminder of the positive results of necessary transformation.

Dagaz has no reversed meaning.

Magical Uses:

Good luck, promote positive transformations, increase in wealth, turning the corner in a challenging situation, spiritual or creative breakthrough

OTHALA

Also known as: Othalan, Othila, Odal, Odhil, Othel
Pronunciation: oh-thee-lah
Letter sound: O (as in "snow")
Translation: inheritance
Keywords: heritage, tradition, inheritance, ancestral property, family ties

Primary Themes

Othala, the final rune of the Elder Futhark, is the rune of heritage, and speaks to what we come into the world with in terms of who we are born to and raised by. This rune may refer to literal inheritance of land or other property, but it is often about the intangible things we "inherit" from our family of origin, for better or worse. No matter how we may resemble or differ from the rest of our family, and no matter how far from home we have traveled or how independently we have established ourselves, all of us carry traits, beliefs, habits and influences from our family of origin.

Drawing Othala may indicate that an aspect of your current situation is related to your background—perhaps unconscious beliefs you absorbed as a child, or some other element that shaped your upbringing.

Like Fehu, the first of the runes, Othala is associated with wealth. However, this is not moveable wealth (such as cattle), but ancestral wealth in the form of land. In ancient Scandinavia, land held within a family could not be sold, but had to be passed down from generation to generation. This practice meant a strong foundation of community, keeping families, clans, and cultural traditions rooted in place. Othala symbolizes these family ties, which were an integral part of life in past centuries, and still are for many people today.

If you live close to your extended family, Othala may be advising you to lean on them for emotional or material support in a challenging matter, or to provide support to a family member in need. This can also be true if you live further away, although in this case the rune could just be nudging you to check in with your people "back home."

In many readings, Othala points to a tension between the traditions you inherited and the current way you're approaching your life. Perhaps you have a lifestyle that your parents and/or ancestors would not approve of, or perhaps you are finding it necessary to hide your true self and conform to the dominant worldview of those around you.

Othala represents a maintaining of the status quo, the way "things have always been done." In an ever-changing world, however, it's up to you to distinguish between what is useful to hang on to, and what needs to be discarded so that you can live and grow in your own authenticity on the physical, emotional, and spiritual levels.

Othala reversed often points to conflict and disharmony within the family, and could indicate a divorce or major rift, or perhaps arguments over inheritance (which is not uncommon when a family member passes on). No matter the source of the dispute, patience and careful observance are recommended, with as much emotional detachment as possible. Avoid aggravating the situation with more discord. Othala reversed may also warn of a loss of property or possessions, or a situation where family support is denied.

More generally, the reversed position indicates a feeling of being alone, isolated from family and/or community, without connection to your current dwelling place. Alternatively, it could be advising you to avoid "rocking the boat" by breaking major family or cultural taboos at this time.

Additional Meanings

Depending on the reading, Othala may also signify assistance from friends or older people. It also may encourage the cultivation of a garden, a particular skill, or an area of study in order to build stable resources. In some instances, it is related to one or more of the querent's past lives.

Magical Uses:

Gaining and holding on to wealth, healing, promote harmonious family relationships, clarity about the self and about the "bigger picture," communication with ancestors

CONCLUSION

As you have no doubt realized by now, the mysteries of the runes defy simple, surface interpretations. Each of these ancient symbols is a wealth of meaning which becomes better understood over time, as you gain more and more experience. Indeed, working with runes can truly become a lifelong journey. There is always more to learn, even for the most advanced rune workers, who understand that the runes will never give up *all* of their secrets.

So don't get discouraged if you don't find instant intuitive connections with every single rune of the Elder Futhark (or any other runic alphabet for that matter). Remember that these mystical relationships take time, as well as dedication. The practice of meditating on one rune per day can be extremely helpful in this regard.

You can start with Fehu and work your way through the Elder Futhark in order, or you can pull one rune per day from your pouch, allowing the runes to guide you toward which one to focus on for the next 24 hours. You may even wish to repeat this process once you've cycled through all of the runes, to deepen your connection to each symbol even further.

A related practice is to allow the runes to help you shape your magical practice. Are you wanting to work rune magic, but not sure which one(s) to use or what goal to work for? Draw one rune from the bag and explore both its divinatory meanings and its magical uses. What might this rune be pointing to that you could use magical assistance with in your life? How might two or three additional runes pulled at random help you see a possible solution more clearly?

When it comes to divination, many people new to runes wonder whether they will be able to read them for friends, family, or even the public in a professional capacity. This choice is up to each individual, but it should be pointed out that runes can be rather trickier to read for others than their more classical counterpart, the Tarot. This is because one's interpretations for the runes can be intensely personal, based on one's own inner worldview and associations with each symbol, which may not translate as easily to someone else's life circumstances.

Furthermore, while Tarot cards are generally image-based, allowing for more intuitive hits to come through for the querent regardless of the querent's familiarity with the cards, runes are quite starkly simple symbols in comparison. Consequently, they generally require more study before divinatory messages become instantly apparent to the querent.

This means that as a reader, you are essentially solely responsible for making meaning out of the reading, with the querent more or less "at the mercy" of your interpretations. This can be a heavy responsibility, since you don't want to inadvertently lead the querent to believe in, and thus create, an undesirable outcome. So by all means, experiment with reading runes for friends if you like, but be sure to approach any reading—whether for yourself or another—from the perspective that the future can always be changed through our choices in the present.

As you become more and more attuned to the energies of the runes, you may also find yourself more drawn to the magical and spiritual traditions of the ancient Germanic peoples. To that end, a list of suggested resources is included at the end of this guide. You'll also find detailed tables of correspondence that can serve as a condensed magical and divinatory guide to the runes of the Elder Futhark. Enjoy these resources, and good luck with your journey into the mysteries of the runes!

SUGGESTIONS FOR FURTHER READING

As discussed in this guide, there are many different approaches to working with runes. Some are firmly rooted within the Germanic magical tradition, while others are not at all. So it shouldn't be surprising that some of the authors on the list below disagree vehemently with each other. Yet each has something valuable to add to the wide array of perspectives on the runes, and so no single approach has been deliberately left out. As always, use your own discernment in selecting your next book on this fascinating topic. Happy reading!

The following authors are generally regarded as working within the context of Northern European magical traditions, drawing from primary historical sources and native lore to a significant degree:

Freya Aswynn, *Principles of Runes* (2000)

Ralph W.V. Elliot, *Runes: an Introduction* (1959)

Bernard King, *Way of the Runes* (2002)

Paul Rhys Mountfort, *Nordic Runes: Understanding, Casting, and Interpreting the Ancient Viking Oracle* (2003)

Nigel Pennick, *Complete Illustrated Guide to Runes* (2002)

Nigel Pennick, *Secrets of the Runes* (1999)

Edred Thorsson, *Futhark: A Handbook of Rune Magic* (1984)

Edred Thorsson, *Runelore: A Handbook of Esoteric Runology* (1987)

Edred Thorsson, *At the Well of Wyrd: A Handbook of Runic Divination* (1988)

These authors may draw on some authentic research into their work, but largely approach the runes from an eclectic, rather than historically-rooted perspective:

Ralph H. Blum, *The Book of Runes* (1983)

Kenneth Meadows, *Rune Power* (1995)

Kaedrich Olsen, *Runes for Transformation: Using Ancient Symbols to Change Your Life* (2008)

Lisa Peschel, *A Practical Guide to the Runes: Their Uses in Divination and Magic* (1989)

Susan Sheppard, *A Witch's Runes: How to Make and Use Your Own Magick Stones* (1998)

For a more developed foundation in Germanic myth and magic, check out any of these sources:

Jackson Crawford, *The Poetic Edda: Stories of the Norse Gods and Heroes* (2015)

Neil Gaiman, *Norse Mythology* (2017)

Nigel Pennick, *Pagan Magic of the Northern Tradition: Customs, Rites, and Ceremonies* (2015)

Snori Sturluson and Jessie Byock, *The Prose Edda: Norse Mythology* (2005)

Edred Thorsson: *Northern Magic: Rune Mysteries and Shamanism* (2002)

RUNIC TABLES OF CORRESPONDENCES

Much of the information in the tables below, such as the names, pronunciations and translations of the runes, is drawn from scholarly sources which are recognized as historically accurate. However, many of the magical correspondences and keywords may come from later, modern developments in runic practice, and are therefore not necessarily representative of how runes were used in ancient Norse religion or magic.

For example, the associated colors may include colors from the Old Norse perception of the rainbow as well as modernly recognized hues. The astrological associations, Elements, and other magical correspondences are drawn from more than one runic system and are not necessarily exhaustive. Use them in spellwork as you see fit, and/or as possible starting places to develop your own system of correspondences for the runes.

Rune	Symbol	Rune Number	Associated Colors	Associated Deities	Astrological Associations	Elements	Misc. Magical Correspondences
Fehu	⊬	1	Brown, gold, light red	Freyr (Frey), Freya	Taurus, Aries, Venus, the Moon	Fire, Earth	Moss agate, amber, elder, nettle
Uruz	⊓	2	Dark green	Thor, Urd, Odin	Taurus, Mars	Water, Earth	Tiger eye, birch, Iceland moss, oak
Thurisaz	⊅	3	White, red	Thor	Mars, Jupiter	Fire	Sapphire, hematite, blackthorn, bramble
Ansuz	⊬	4	Purple, dark blue, red	Odin, Loki, Eostre	Venus, Mercury, Libra	Air	Emerald, lapis lazuli, ash, hazel
Raidho	⊭	5	Blue, bright red	Ing, Nerthus	Sagittarius, Mercury	Air	Turquoise, oak, mugwort, holly
Kenaz	∨	6	Yellow, light red, orange	Heimdall, Freyja, Frey	Venus, Mars, the Sun	Fire	Bloodstone, amber, smoky quartz, pine, cowslip
Gebo	✕	7	Blue, deep green	Odin, Gefn	Pisces, Venus	Air, Water	Opal, jade, elm, ash, apple, heartsease
Wunjo	⊳	8	Yellow, purple	Odin, Frigg, Frey	Leo, Mars, Venus, Saturn	Water, Earth	Diamond, rose quartz, ivy, ash, flax

Rune	Symbol	Rune Number	Associated Colors	Associated Deities	Astrological Associations	Elements	Misc. Magical Correspondences
Hagalaz		9	White, light blue	Hagal, Heimdall, Urd	Aquarius, Saturn	Water, Ice	Jet, onyx, elder, nightshade, yew
Nauthiz		10	Blue, black	Urd, Verdandi, Skuld (the Norns)	Capricorn, Saturn	Fire	Lapis lazuli, rowan, beech
Isa		11	White, black	Verdandi	The Moon, Jupiter	Water, Ice	Cat's eye, blackthorn, henbane, beech, alder
Jera		12	Brown, light blue, green	Frey, Freyja	The Sun, Mercury	Earth	Carnelian, moss agate, oak, rosemary
Eihwaz		13	Green, dark blue	Ullr, Odin	Scorpio, Venus, Jupiter	Air	Topaz, smoky quartz, yew, mandrake, hemlock
Perthro		14	Red, black, white	Frigg, the Norns	Saturn, Mars	Water	Aquamarine, onyx, beech, elder, yew
Elhaz		15	Purple, gold	Heimdall	Cancer	Air, Fire, Water	Black tourmaline, Iceland spar, rowan, angelica, yew
Sowilo		16	Yellow, white, gold	Baldur	The Sun	Fire	Ruby, sunstone, juniper, mistletoe

Rune	Symbol	Rune Number	Associated Colors	Associated Deities	Astrological Associations	Elements	Misc. Magical Correspondences
Tiwaz	↑	17	Red	Tyr	Mars, Libra	Air	Bloodstone, hematite, coral, oak, sage
Berkana	ᛒ	18	Blue, dark green	Nerthus, Holda, the Birch Goddess	Jupiter, the Moon, Virgo	Earth	Moonstone, jet, birch, alchemilla
Ehwaz	ᛖ	19	White, red, orange	Frey, Freya	Gemini, Mercury	Earth, Water	Iceland spar, turquoise, ragwort, oak, ash
Mannaz	ᛗ	20	Purple, deep red	Heimdall, Odin, Frigg	Jupiter	Earth, Air	Garnet, amethyst, holly, elm, ash
Laguz	↙	21	Green, blue-green	Niord, Nerthus	The Moon	Water	Pearl, malachite, willow, leek
Ingwaz	⋈	22	Black, yellow	Ing, Frey	Venus, Cancer	Fire, Earth	Amber, quartz, apple, self-heal
Dagaz	ᛞ	23	Yellow, light blue	Heimdall	The Sun	Fire, Water, Air	Chrysolite, fluorite, spruce, clary sage
Othala	◇	24	Yellow, gold, green	Odin	Saturn, Mars	Earth	Star ruby, moss agate, oak, hawthorn

RUNIC LETTERS TO
ENGLISH CONVERSION CHART

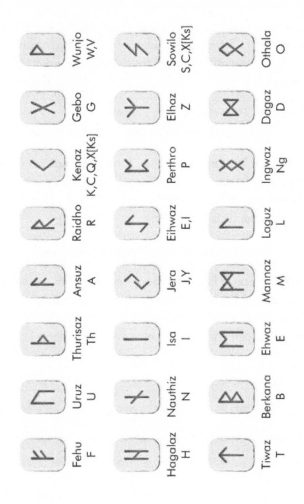

Wunjo — W, V
Gebo — G
Kenaz — K, C, Q, X[Ks]
Raidho — R
Ansuz — A
Thurisaz — Th
Uruz — U
Fehu — F

Sowilo — S, C, X[Ks]
Elhaz — Z
Perthro — P
Eihwaz — E, I
Jera — J, Y
Isa — I
Nauthiz — N
Hagalaz — H

Othala — O
Dagaz — D
Ingwaz — Ng
Laguz — L
Mannaz — M
Ehwaz — E
Berkana — B
Tiwaz — T

FREE AUDIOBOOK PROMOTION

Don't forget, you can now enjoy a **free audiobook** when you start a free 30-day trial with Audible.

If you're interested in divination, *Runes for Beginners* is a great bet, with a thorough introduction to the origins and meanings of these ancient mystical symbols, including their divinatory interpretations and their uses in magic. Download for free here:

www.wiccaliving.com/free-runes-audiobook

Or, if you'd like to learn another form of divination, *Tarot for Beginners* covers the origins of Tarot, a comprehensive overview of the 78 cards and their meanings, and tips for beginning readers. Simply visit:

www.wiccaliving.com/free-tarot-audiobook

Members receive free audiobooks every month, as well as exclusive discounts. And, if you don't want to continue with Audible, just remember to cancel your membership. You won't be charged a cent, and you'll get to keep your books!

Happy listening!

MORE BOOKS BY
LISA CHAMBERLAIN

Wicca for Beginners: A Guide to Wiccan Beliefs, Rituals, Magic, and Witchcraft

Wicca Book of Spells: A Book of Shadows for Wiccans, Witches, and Other Practitioners of Magic

Wicca Herbal Magic: A Beginner's Guide to Practicing Wiccan Herbal Magic, with Simple Herb Spells

Wicca Book of Herbal Spells: A Book of Shadows for Wiccans, Witches, and Other Practitioners of Herbal Magic

Wicca Candle Magic: A Beginner's Guide to Practicing Wiccan Candle Magic, with Simple Candle Spells

Wicca Book of Candle Spells: A Book of Shadows for Wiccans, Witches, and Other Practitioners of Candle Magic

Wicca Crystal Magic: A Beginner's Guide to Practicing Wiccan Crystal Magic, with Simple Crystal Spells

Wicca Book of Crystal Spells: A Book of Shadows for Wiccans, Witches, and Other Practitioners of Crystal Magic

Tarot for Beginners: A Guide to Psychic Tarot Reading, Real Tarot Card Meanings, and Simple Tarot Spreads

Runes for Beginners: A Guide to Reading Runes in Divination, Rune Magic, and the Meaning of the Elder Futhark Runes

Wicca Moon Magic: A Wiccan's Guide and Grimoire for Working Magic with Lunar Energies

Wicca Wheel of the Year Magic: A Beginner's Guide to the Sabbats, with History, Symbolism, Celebration Ideas, and Dedicated Sabbat Spells

Wicca Kitchen Witchery: A Beginner's Guide to Magical Cooking, with Simple Spells and Recipes

Wicca Essential Oils Magic: A Beginner's Guide to Working with Magical Oils, with Simple Recipes and Spells

Wicca Elemental Magic: A Guide to the Elements, Witchcraft, and Magical Spells

Wicca Magical Deities: A Guide to the Wiccan God and Goddess, and Choosing a Deity to Work Magic With

Wicca Living a Magical Life: A Guide to Initiation and Navigating Your Journey in the Craft

Magic and the Law of Attraction: A Witch's Guide to the Magic of Intention, Raising Your Frequency, and Building Your Reality

Wicca Altar and Tools: A Beginner's Guide to Wiccan Altars, Tools for Spellwork, and Casting the Circle

Wicca Finding Your Path: A Beginner's Guide to Wiccan Traditions, Solitary Practitioners, Eclectic Witches, Covens, and Circles

Wicca Book of Shadows: A Beginner's Guide to Keeping Your Own Book of Shadows and the History of Grimoires

Modern Witchcraft and Magic for Beginners: A Guide to Traditional and Contemporary Paths, with Magical Techniques for the Beginner Witch

FREE GIFT REMINDER

Just a reminder that Lisa is giving away an exclusive, free spell book as a thank-you gift to new readers!

Little Book of Spells contains ten spells that are ideal for newcomers to the practice of magic, but are also suitable for any level of experience.

Read it on read on your laptop, phone, tablet, Kindle or Nook device by visiting:

www.wiccaliving.com/bonus

DID YOU ENJOY
RUNES FOR BEGINNERS?

Thanks so much for reading this book! I know there are many great books out there about the runes, so I really appreciate you choosing this one.

If you enjoyed the book, I have a small favor to ask—would you take a couple of minutes to leave a review for this book on Amazon?

Your feedback will help me to make improvements to this book, and to create even better ones in the future. It will also help me develop new ideas for books on other topics that might be of interest to you. Thanks in advance for your help!

Made in the USA
Monee, IL
27 December 2020

55671985R00080